How to Be Happy Partners:
Working It Out Together

By

Tina B. Tessina, PhD and
Riley K. Smith, MA

Muffinhaven Press Long Beach, California

Muffinhaven Press, Long Beach, CA
Library of Congress Cataloging-in-Publication
Data Tessina, Tina B. and Smith, Riley K.

How to Be Happy Partners
ISBN-13: 978-1530583591 (CreateSpace-Assigned)
ISBN-10: 1530583594

BISAC: Family & Relationships / Marriage &
Long Term Relationships

10 9 8 7 6 5 4 3 2 1
Original Edition 2016

Acknowledgments

Tina B. Tessina: No one but a writer's spouse knows what patience and tolerance he must have to hang in there. My husband, Richard Sharrard, has all that and more. His unflagging love and support are a miracle in my life. He knows how to be a loveable child and a passionate adult, and when to be which. My love, thanks for so many moments, words, thoughts, and gestures in the last 36 years. Thanks to my co- author, the multi-talented Riley K. Smith, who also designed the cover, and he is always a delightful writing partner. Literary Agent Laurie Harper, who has been a dynamo and an amazing support in my career. Joyful thanks to the cosmic support team, in (more or less) alphabetical order: Isadora Alman, Maggie and Ed Bialack, Victoria Bryan, and Sylvia and Glen Mc Williams, who listened with interest, encouraged me with affectionate phone calls, and even got me away from it all. You guys are my soul support, and life would be a lot less fun without you. Also to Jean Marie Stine, Jeremy Tarcher and Al Saunders, the publishers who first took an interest in me and thought I could do it.

Table of Contents

Introduction

If you are struggling to find lasting satisfaction in your intimate relationships, you're not alone. Like the many couples we have worked with, you may be struggling with your partner, searching for a way to be happy together. You may have…

- experienced a sequence of relationships that were destructive and didn't work.
- a chance with someone new and fear you will repeat old, painful patterns.
- a basically good relationship with some specific problems (such as financial struggles, disagreements about parenting, sex, intimacy, housework or time schedules) for which you can't find a satisfactory solution.
- fights all the time and are unable to resolve even minor family problems or conflicts without a painful and exasperating struggle, which leaves one or both of you feeling hurt, angry, resentful, deprived, cheated, or frustrated.
- thought that you have to choose between taking a stand for yourself and having a committed relationship, because you can't have both at the same time.

If you have had experiences such as these you are not alone. Many couples have trouble sustaining a long-term intimate relationship. In our long experience as counselors and also in our own relationships, we have discovered the secret to getting along with each other, and still having what you want. When you feel free to speak up and say what you want, confident that you will be heard and confident that your partner will work with you to find a solution, love will flow more easily between you, and you can both be happy in different ways.

Compromise and Competition

Traditionally, relationships were built on specific roles for each partner, which invited compromise and competition, resentment and struggle. If your relationship is based on compromise or competition, you will struggle:

- One makes too many compromises to please the other, he or she becomes a resentful caretaker, while the other feels oppressed and belittled
- One of you may be alert to the moods of the other, often walking on eggshells not to upset your partner. The other may threaten to leave in order to get his or her way.
- One of you wants more together time and the other wants more space, and neither is satisfied with the compromise.
- Relationships based on compromising or placating are full of resentment, hurt, pain and power struggles.

Struggling and resenting each other can block the flow of love between you, even when you truly love one another. When you know how to communicate and cooperate as equals, you can create a deeply treasured loving partnership and be committed to equality and mutual satisfaction.

This book is a how-to manual you can use to create or restructure your current relationship into a happy partnership. There are many tools and techniques, step-by-step instructions and guidelines in these pages which you and your partner can use to create cooperation and freedom (including The Negotiation Tree, a tool that can help you turn any struggle into a cooperative problem-solving session.)

The definition of what a relationship is has gone through massive changes in recent times. More people are choosing not to marry, or not to stay married, today. Instead, they are redefining couple relationships in many ways. The trouble is that many relationship books offer patterns based on old models and do not recognize the changes that have taken place. Your relationship is unique, and you need to work together to create a partnership in which both of you can be happy as individuals, yet loving and committed as a couple.

How to Be Happy Partners is designed to help you create a relationship that works for you, whether your relationship is traditionally monogamous; gay or straight; or non-traditional, a bi-coastal, two-career relationship; or a committed, living-separately relationship. There are many possible variations of satisfying relationships, and this book is about creating the kind of relationship that satisfies you and your partner.

Whatever kind of relationship you want, you and your partner can use the tools here to develop your own mutually satisfying definition, which is specific to your individual relationship, whether you are dating, living together, married, or not married. Whether you want a deep emotional and sexual commitment or something lighter, we can help you and your partner achieve your own, unique and specific style of relationship. How to Be Happy Partners will help you sustain it and be happy in it.

Space and Closeness

You and your partner have different needs for closeness and personal space, as well as other needs to feel nurtured, understood, and autonomous within your relationship. Some of you may want to be close and comforted; others want to be autonomous and unfettered. It's not unusual to want both at the same time.

Reconciling your different wants requires self-knowledge. To know what you need, you must see yourself as clearly as possible and accept what you find there. Knowing what you want and what you feel are skills that are essential to creating a mutually satisfying intimate relationship; and we give you tools specific exercises designed to help you clarify what you want and feel, to create a personal definition of freedom, and to communicate that to your partner. These techniques help you create mutual understanding and cooperation in working as partners to get exactly what each of you wants.

Whether your reasons for wanting to be a couple are romantic or pragmatic, social or cultural, based on passion or a need to create a healthier family than you grew up in, a desire to have children, simple loneliness, or a spiritual or soul mate connection, we want to help you create it as you see it.

The Desire for Intimacy

Most couples are drawn together because they crave intimacy. Yet differences in how to define intimacy is also what creates most of the struggle in relationships. Creating a satisfying couple relationship requires meeting both of your individual intimacy needs.

You need intimacy just as you need food and shelter. Just as with the other basic needs, no one needs intimacy all the time, but some people need more than others. It is possible to be intimate without being a couple; however, the development of emotional closeness over time combined with the easy availability of physical closeness, make couple relationships the ideal opportunity for intimate contact. When you are recognized partners, building intimacy is easier because it takes less energy and decision-making to get together. Friends, family, and culture support and endorse your togetherness.

When things go well, the teamwork of partnership (common goals, successfully solving daily problems, and doing chores together) creates a feeling of mutuality and app recitation that enhances your closeness. As a couple, you are freed from the search for intimacy, so you can focus on other areas of your lives. In a healthy relationship, intimacy grows with time. Two people who have been together for 20 years can have a deeper connection than they did when they were only dating for three months.

Time together doesn't guarantee intimacy, but it does create an opportunity for intimacy to grow. It takes time to know and trust each other. As trust builds, you open yourselves. Over the months (or years), you reveal yourselves. If you nurture your closeness through the years of each partner's personal growth and changes, you will know more about each other than anyone else, and your contact will grow deep.

Once you learn the communication and problem-solving skills in this book, you'll know how to create the kind of teamwork and mutual benefit that supports the growth of intimacy and satisfaction: a relationship of happy partnership and autonomous cooperation.

Cooperative Problem Solving

Most people don't believe that it is possible for a couple to be so adept at solving problems together that both of them are fully satisfied. The myth is that you must choose between intimacy and freedom: that is, you can have what you want, or you can be close. Couple relationships are seen as an extension of other types of competition. Because this competitive attitude is so ingrained in each of us, it usually takes a shift in belief and a lot of practice to learn how to stop fighting, arguing, and insisting you are right; or to stop being afraid you won't get what you want.

Happy Partners

Happy partners embody five qualities:
1) love easily expressed,
2) mutual respect,
3) a sense of equal power in the relationship,
4) the willingness and ability to express desires, needs, satisfaction, and
5) the willingness and ability to resolve conflicts cooperatively without power plays, manipulation, and unsatisfying compromises.

How to Be Happy Partners will teach you to work together to create whatever kind of relationship you want, free from the restrictive patterns of your parents, your past experience, and social pressures.

When you and your partner know how to cooperate to solve problems and resolve differences, both of you:
- can freely express your desires, needs, and satisfactions.
- can share your worries and your joy without fear of being manipulated by them.

- feel equally empowered.
- ask for what you want, knowing you will work together to make it happen.
- experience and express mutual respect, so love flows more easily between you.
- understand how to cooperate to create a truly satisfying life as two free individuals working together.
- be happy partners, satisfied and secure.

Emphasizing Function Rather Than Dysfunction

If you want to know "What is a healthy, functional relationship and how do we get one?" How to Be Happy Partners is designed to answer your questions and teach you (either individually or together with your partner) how to create and sustain a fully functioning partnership between equals.

How to Be Happy Partners is a manual that provides intimate partners with a proven, step-by-step guide for working together as a team to overcome negative relationship patterns and master the positive new skills you'll need to know to create a successful, satisfying, and sustainable relationship that fulfils both your individual needs. The exercises in this book have been used and recommended by many therapists to help couples in therapy

The central idea of this book is a method for Cooperative Problem Solving that involves both partners working together as a team. Through this process, any problems, difficulties, obstacles, differences, or struggles that arise can be identified, negotiated, and solved to the mutual satisfaction of you and your partner.

This book will lead you, individually as well as together, through a series of carefully planned exercises designed to help you develop the skills (such as problem-solving, cooperation, clear communication, and teamwork) that will enable you to use the cooperative problem solving process to build and sustain a healthy relationship.

In How to Be Happy Partners you will learn how to work together smoothly to solve the very problems that created competition, pain, and struggle between you and your partner in the past and to build teamwork and cooperation where you previously had fighting, frustration, and despair. Your problems are probably solvable; relationship problems feel overwhelming and difficult only if the partners involved lack the skills they need to solve them.

The basis of this approach is The Negotiation Tree: A step-by-step guide to working smoothly together to solve all the problems and disputes partners can encounter over the course of a relationship. It will guide you safely through the five steps of solving any problem and help the two of you reach a solution that is wholly and non-competitively satisfying to you both.

This book will introduce you to a model of a happy partnership:

- Designed to meet your unique needs as individuals and as a couple.
- In which both partners feel equally important, equally powerful, and equally free to express their wants and needs.
- In which both partners work together to find a mutually satisfactory way to get what both of you want every single time.
- In which you support each other in making sure you are both satisfied in the relationship.
- Which contains far less conflict, frustration, anger, and fewer arguments, disputes, and feelings of deprivation than most couples experience.
- Which is easy to sustain because you both learn how to get what you want from it all the time.

Chapter One

How to Be Happy Partners

Fights about money, sex, affection, time, infidelity, in-laws, raising children, housekeeping, or other problems which don't to reach a mutually agreeable or satisfying solution mean you are repeating the same old arguments. You are locked in habitual ways of relating which are familiar and create dissatisfaction and struggle between you.

The skills (communication, cooperation, understanding and asking for what you want, overcoming destructive habits, breaking out of rigid patterns that don't work, counteracting entrenched habits and creating new ideas to solve problems together successfully) in here are what you need to work together as a team rather than struggle against each other. The steps in The Negotiation Tree will keep you on track and prevent you from sliding back into old habits.

Like the couples you'll follow in this book, you may have had relationships that frequently felt more like nightmares than dreams; struggling with different wants and needs; not knowing how to work together effectively to solve the conflict, and winding up feeling resulting frustration, anger and battles which made things more and more unpleasant and closeness difficult to sustain.

Most relationships we can observe: our parents, extended family, neighbors and friends, and on movies and TV, seem to be full of struggle, pain, and boredom and fraught with problems:

- one partner gives and the other takes,
- one is an addict, alcoholic or gambler and the other pays the price,
- one partner overpowers, coerces, defrauds, deceives, or takes advantage of the other,
- they both follow rigid roles that seem to alter or stifle their personalities,
- one gives up a career to support a spouse who succeeds, then leaves,
- both partners seem filled with anger, contempt, hostility, or hatred of the other,
- both compromise their needs for the survival of the marriage,
- they both withhold their true thoughts and feelings because "my partner wouldn't like it", and feel dissatisfied,
- one or both are numb, depressed, or detached, and they are partners only in that they cohabitate, or they stay together for the children or because they feel they have to,
- the romance is gone and there is no vitality,
- their sexual needs and differences seem to conflict, creating emotional suffering for both, or
- one or both have affairs to fill a missing ingredient in their partnership.

But there is hope. Cooperative problem solving and The Negotiation Tree can help you learn to work out happy solutions to problems like these, by working together to ensure each other's satisfaction. For any problem is too severe or long-standing to be solved by mutual discussion, this book will show you when and how to seek help, and simultaneously show you how to make room in your relationship for individual differences, preferences and tastes.

You can have a successful Happy Partnership even when there are still some personal emotional problems you have not resolved. Working together, you can help each other overcome individual problems, (whether they are emotional, from past history, work-related or stem from some other part of your separate lives) and you can make enough room in your relationship that your moods and personalities can co-exist without undue struggle. As you develop more mutuality and cooperation, your relationship will improve in an ever-increasing spiral.

Cooperative problem solving offers you an easy-to-follow, effective, non-competitive method to help you work together to:

- recognize and solve problems in your relationship, whether you've been together for a long time, or you are a newly committed couple.

- keep your individual problems from creating partnership problems,

- solve each other's individual problems to your mutual satisfaction.

- solve your relationship problems to your mutual satisfaction.

- review the interaction in your past relationships to learn what went wrong, identify behavior and beliefs that got in your way before, and correct them.

- identify old relationship patterns that were dysfunctional, addictive or abusive, and to develop healthy interaction.

- discuss changing or conflicting individual moods and feelings, or different needs for intimacy, and find ways to accommodate them.

- identify and examine the traditional relationship models to see what aspects of them are relevant to your partnership, and what you need to change.

- develop a model for partnership, no matter what your style, orientation, or preference, that works for you and your mate, and learn the skills you need to be whole, healthy, independent individuals who have satisfying, loving intimacy as equal partners.

Decision Making: It Takes Equals to Solve Problems

When you believe that somehow happy couples just agree on everything automatically all the time, you enter relationships convinced that whatever problems or differences you have will be easy to solve. But we soon find otherwise: because it's normal for you and your partner to disagree and struggle over even minor issues.

It's not easy to build and sustain a lifetime relationship; and you are bound to encounter problems. Different backgrounds and experience, individual perception of each other and events, unequal history of education and growth, individual needs for self-expression and contact, and differing values and beliefs about relationships complicate and often block our attempts at cooperative problem solving together.

Complicating all this is the fact that models of healthy, effective problem solving between partners in a relationship are rare. For centuries, the accepted models for intimate, business and political relationships were authoritarian, with a parental boss (usually male) in charge who made all the critical decisions and passed them down to subordinates (often female) who accomplished them without question.

Although it may sometimes work in business, relationships based on the idea that one person must lead and the other follow (one win and the other lose) become power struggles, where the partners fight bitterly when they disagree because they struggle to be in control, or avoid disagreements altogether because it isn't worth the struggle, or they'd lose anyway. Thus, they spend a lot of their time either fighting for what they want or feeling deprived. You may have witnessed your parents, friends or neighbors interacting in this way, because competitive relationships have been the norm.

Competition and Winning

The belief that someone has to win in a relationship encourages us to compete rather than to cooperate. As children we learn (when the teacher favors a brighter student, or a sister who is more assertive gets to decide the game we'll play) if we aren't the best, don't fight hard, or manipulate we don't get what we want, which leads us to either struggle for it, or give up.

Partners try to win, because in competition, only one person gets satisfied. Most of us are used to competing for jobs, sports, dates, and we even compete with ourselves, to see if we can outdo our previous efforts. When competition is stimulating, motivating and fun, it is healthy.

Competition between intimate partners becomes stressful, counter-productive and toxic, poisoning the relationship by turning us into adversaries, and undermining the mutual support and encouragement vital to becoming Happy Partners.

Fear of Difference

Another reason resolving problems and conflicts with an intimate partner can be difficult is the closeness of loving intimacy. When you have an intimate, bonded relationship, disagreements seem threatening. Differing indicates you are separate individuals who perceive everything differently and have different needs and wants, and that creates fear that you'll be rejected or disapproved of if you differ. Reluctance to disrupt the intimacy leads to handling problems or disagreements clumsily, and often makes the problem worse.

Outside Problem

Sometimes relationship problems are only indirectly connected to your partnership: your car breaks down, your kids need to get to school, or the boss is difficult to get along with. These issues become partnership problems because you bring their effects, big and small, home with you. Anger at your unreasonable boss can quickly become a difficult evening with your partner if you bring your frustration home, are irritable, and the two of you wind up arguing unnecessarily, not even understanding why.

This may feel unfair and inappropriate, but in real life it happens frequently. When you and your partner don't have the skills to work together to identify and solve problems, you can easily become tangled in a web of blaming, hurt and anger and, after years of similar unresolved conflicts, you can create a backlog of bitterness which is resistant to healing.

Relationship Disagreements

Sometimes problems are directly related to your relationship: you fight about housework or money, you have conflicts over sex. One or both of you becomes hurt or angry. At these times, if you don't know how to work together to solve the problem, the conflict and the resulting negative feelings can easily escalate or accumulate over time, coming up over and over because they never get resolved, and undermine an otherwise loving and viable partnership.

Struggling and believing you can't both have what you want prevents you from reaching a good resolution. If you believe that you're not going to get what you want because:

- there isn't enough to go around,
- you don't deserve it as much as your partner,
- it will be taken away from you, or
- it isn't nice to want

…then you aren't going to believe there you can get what you want. When disagreements or difficulties arise, if you feel hopeless, panicked and angry or confused, you aren't thinking clearly enough to solve the problem.

Effective Decision Making

Only recently have psychologists and sociologists begun to discuss the elements of effective decision making. Research shows that decision making (even in business) is more effective when everyone contributes their views of priorities, needs, wants, goals, and their thoughts about possible solutions. This cooperative approach means that everyone contributes their understanding to the problem (which often makes it clearer) and everyone feels involved in the process and committed to the success of the solution agreed on.

If, up to now, you viewed negotiation in a relationship as a struggle or a hassle, an opportunity to be overpowered or cheated, you are not alone. Because we live in a competitive society, where a lot of emphasis is placed on winning or losing a conflict, it is difficult to realize that, when we are dealing with those we love, problems can be solved through cooperative teamwork, and that solutions can be reached where no one loses, and everyone benefits.

How to Be Happy Partners will help you learn a new way of working out the daily difficulties and decisions involved in becoming an effective, supportive, smooth-working team who work together for mutual satisfaction.

Read further and you will learn an effective, proven model for resolving your inevitable relationship difficulties which is called Cooperative Problem Solving. You can use this method to resolve a conflict or make a decision and negotiate matters so that both of you get what you want. Here you can learn all the highly effective decision making skills you need to solve each relationship problem as it arises. You can learn how to solve the problems of the past (I'm afraid we'll fight about money like my first wife and I did); the present (I don't think I'm getting a fair share of the housework) and the future (what will we do if I lose my job?). Instead of being a struggle or something to avoid; solving such problems will become an opportunity to reaffirm your mutual love and caring, and to strengthen your partnership and teamwork.

How to Be Happy Partners is a step-by-step guide to help you learn how to move easily together through the five simple steps of Cooperative Problem Solving, using The Negotiation Tree.

Cooperative Problem Solving

Cooperation means working together as equals, focused on solving the problem in a way that satisfies of your needs. Using Cooperative Problem Solving, you solve problems working together, rather than struggling with each other, so all of your emotional, mental, and creative energy can be focused on finding a solution, creatively exploring the problem, developing alternatives, putting your mutually chosen solutions into action, and agreeing on a solution.

When you and your partner want different things, you can argue over who is right (the winner) or wrong (the loser) in order to have your way. or give up convinced it is not worth it or you can never win over your partner and feel restricted, deprived, hurt and angry.

Carol and Joe

Carol and Joe, for example, have a conflict. They both want the car for the evening. Because of their conflicting wants, they get anxious that there might not be enough transportation for the two of them, and begin arguing. Carol (after arguing about who needs or deserves the car more for about 20 minutes) gets angry enough to grab the keys and take the car, leaving Joe to find other transportation. Carol has won the car, but created a bigger relationship problem: Joe ends up feeling deprived and angry and Carol feels anxious and guilty.

Because they are convinced there is no way both of them can have what they want, they get upset and fight, so neither of them considers an alternate solution, and someone has to do without transportation.

On the other hand, if Carol and Joe learn to solve problems as partners, they will together as a team to reach a mutually happy solution. Confident that both of them be content with the result, they will be much less likely to approach the transportation problem with a win or lose attitude, and both will be more willing to be flexible, accepting and understanding of each other.

As partners, Carol and Joe now focus on finding a way for both to get transportation for the evening, consider other options (Joe can get a ride with a neighbor, relative or friend, Carol can drop Joe off on her way, either can take a taxi, ride-hail, bus or a train, someone else may let them borrow a car, they can adjust their schedules so they don't need the car at the same time, or they might even decide to rent or buy another car) and negotiate until they both are satisfied.

The negotiation techniques you will learn here are based on the belief that both of you are right and deserve to have what you want.

When you follow the exercises and guidelines you will see how to find a solution that satisfies both of you. You will discover that it is indeed possible for both you and your partner to have exactly what you want and learn the skills you need to get it.

Cooperative problem solving is a new way of looking at decision making, agreements, communication, power sharing, and solving problems; a way to replace your competitive interaction with teamwork and cooperation; and the fear that you will lose what you want with confidence that both of you can be satisfied. You can use these ideas and exercises, to create teamwork and equal partnership in your intimate relationship.

In five simple steps, cooperative problem solving presents a method of resolving conflict based on better understanding of each other's wants and needs, communicating clearly, developing new, creative options, making decisions, and reaching solutions that are completely satisfactory to both partners. Cooperative problem solving will help you master the basic attitudes and skills of cooperation at the same time as it helps you to solve your problems.

Cooperative problem solving also motivates you and your partner to participate equally and actively in resolving struggles because its goal is to help you develop a solution that completely satisfies both of you. The specific options, such as how to clarify and communicate the problem, how to make sure your partner is equally involved, and what to do when your partner doesn't want to cooperate will help you solve existing problems while simultaneously teaching you skills you can use in the future. You are about to develop the skills to create a partnership that meets both your needs, desires and aspirations; in which the daily problems and decisions of living are smoothly and easily handled, because you know how to successfully find solutions instead of competing.

If you cooperate to solve problems when they arise, the experience of working together and caring about each other's wants (Joe and Carol mutually decide that Carol will drop Joe off, so they both have transportation) builds trust and goodwill between you. This feeling of mutual trust, (the next negotiation about the car will be easier, and Carol and Joe will be more relaxed, because they cooperated this time) and confidence that you can successfully meet challenges together, creates a solid bond between you, and is the key to establishing a Happy Partnership.

Cooperative problem solving will help you solve problems:

- When you know what you want, but you're not getting it.
- If you know you're unhappy, but aren't sure what you want.
- If your partner is obviously unhappy and you don't know why.
- When you and your partner seriously disagree over what you want or how to handle a problem.

Each time you have a partnership decision to make, from buying a new car or house to deciding parenting issues or whose career move is most beneficial. The chapters and the exercises will quickly show you and your partner which negotiation problems arise most often for you, which skills you need to practice, and which attitudes have kept you stuck in your past relationship problems. The skills and the guidelines in The Negotiation Tree will become easier and flow more naturally as you do them, because you'll overcome barriers and develop new skills for communication and conflict resolving and correct old competitive attitudes as you work through them.

Barriers and Skills

As you begin to learn and work with the five steps of cooperative problem solving you will learn many new skills, and probably encounter a number of difficulties that will tempt you to give up and abandon the process. We call these difficulties the barriers to cooperative problem solving. Each chapter outlines the typical barriers, such as:

- not knowing what you want,
- competing,
- inexperience and mistrust,

- confusion,
- lack of communication,
- not enough information, and
- unresolved anger...

...you are likely to encounter at each step of the process.

It then teaches you specific skills such as:

- Clarifying Your Wants,
- Cooperation,
- Reassurance,
- Clear Communication,
- Research Projects, and
- Discharging Old Anger

...Which are designed to overcome them.

The Negotiation Tree will teach you and your partner the skills you need:

- to be aware of the possible barriers,
- to anticipate them and minimize the problems they cause, and
- to overcome the barriers you do encounter as you learn cooperative problem solving.

Cooperation and Happy Partnership

Happy Partnership is the long-range benefit of learning to problem-solve in this way. By using the cooperative problem solving tools to resolve several problems in a totally satisfying way, you will begin to feel more secure about your teamwork, and therefore, your partnership. Knowing you can make agreements that both of you will keep, and that when problems arise you can work together to solve them, will build a deeper level of trust between you:

- trust that you can handle life's difficulties, problems and disagreements in a spirit of cooperation,
- trust that you both are willing to work for your mutual satisfaction, and

- trust that you really care about each other's happiness as well as your own

Communication and negotiating skills are useful everywhere: at work, and dealing with children, other family members and friends, because the same techniques that make it easier to work together with your partner also ease all other attempts at communication.

When you learn how to present a problem clearly in a way that invites your partner to work on it with you, you will be able to use the same method to address a problem with coworkers. Conflicts resulting from misunderstandings become rare and when they do arise they are far more easily resolved in every part of your life.

Over time, this new way of relating as equals who work together can transform your relationship, as it did with Joe and Carol. They realized through cooperative problem solving (becoming more clear about what they wanted, working to understand each other, and seeking mutually satisfactory solutions), that Joe needed to learn to take better care of himself and Carol, who knew how to care for Joe, was learning to be aware of her own needs.

As they learned this new mutually caring attitude through solving simple problems such as who got the car, their way of being together changed. At first, Carol asked for more affection and help with the housework. Joe agreed and asked for help learning what she wanted so he could be warm and caring toward her, and to take more responsibility around the house.

As they negotiated successfully through a long series of small adjustments over a period of months, they also modified how they behaved toward each other. Joe learned to share his dissatisfaction with his work, and be more affectionate toward Carol, and Carol felt more responsive and generous to Joe as she learned get her own needs met.

As a result of working together on these and other related issues, Joe was encouraged to get training for a new, more satisfying and better paying career, and Carol became more independent, and had more time and energy for her career. They learned to cooperate on housekeeping chores, until they became successful enough that they hired a housekeeper. Their mutual support and lack of struggle at home reduced their stress and gave them an extra boost in their careers, and both thrived as a result.

The accumulated positive experience of Cooperative problem solving helps you work together successfully to meet the challenges of life and living as a team, and the confidence and mutual trust resulting from success creates a solid bond between you (the more problems Carol and Joe solve successfully, the more the warmth and trust between them grows).

Couples who know from experience that they can successfully make decisions and that they can feel mutually satisfied and enhanced by being with each other, do not doubt their relationship or their commitment. When a relationship goes well, the reasons for being in it are clear: Why would anyone want to leave a relationship where they get what they want all the time? The Negotiation Tree will help you work together until you have enough experience that you automatically seek to find mutually satisfying solutions to every problem that arises, and you can build this kind of solid, reliable happy partnership.

The Negotiation Tree

Although the five steps of Cooperative problem solving are simple, we realize there will be many occasions especially when you are first beginning to learn to use it, when you will get stuck, not know what to do or fall back into unhealthy old patterns like competition, arguing, not knowing what you want, misunderstanding each other, or feeling discouraged or confused. At such times you will need help in staying focused on Cooperative problem solving, or you may find that your negotiation winds up in argument and frustration rather than solving the problem.

To help ease you through such difficulty and speed you back on the right track, we have developed The Negotiation Tree, a blue print for problem solving, or a road map that will help guide you, with tested and proven methods, through the problems of problem solving.

It is based on the decision tree: a decision support tool that uses a tree-like graph or model of decisions and their possible consequences. Decision trees are excellent tools for helping you to choose between several courses of action. They provide a highly effective structure within which you can lay out options and investigate the possible outcomes of choosing those options.

We call ours the Negotiation Tree because it describes all the steps of cooperative negotiation, with "if yes" and "if no" branches that help you understand 1) where you are in the negotiation, 2) if it is going well, and 3) what you need to do next. It also contains references to whatever skill you may need at any point, and which exercise in the book teaches the skill.

You will want to refer to it often, so you may want to make a copy of it for easy reference.

THE NEGOTIATION TREE

Step I: Define and Communicate Your Problem:

Is the Problem Clear to You?

If yes,	If no,
State your problem to your partner, get confirmation that it is understood, and proceed to Step II.	Can your partner help clarify the problem by discussing it?

If yes,	If no,
Discuss problem until it is defined then proceed to Step II.	Do it yourself by:

_____

Example of Stating Problem:

"I'm feeling neglected and needy lately because you're gone so much."

_____

1. Doing the Problem Inventory in Chapter 2

2. If still unclear, read Chapter 2, Define and Communicate the Problem.

3. If still unclear, do the Clarifying Your Wants exercise in Chapter 5

4. If still unclear, get help from a friend or therapist

Step II: Agree To Negotiate.

Do You Both Agree To Negotiate?

If yes,	If no,
Proceed to Step III.	1. Reassure your partner or ask for reassurance for yourself, as appropriate. Follow the Guidelines for Reassurance in Chapter 3.
Example of Asking to Negotiate:	2. If still no agreement, review Chapter 3, Agree to Negotiate, and do the Trouble Shooting Guide in Chapter 3.
"Will you sit down with me and help me solve this problem?"	3. If still no agreement, persist using the Guidelines for Gentle Persistence, Chapter 3.
	4. If still no agreement, solve it your self using Guidelines for Solving It Yourself in Chapter 3

Step III: Set the Stage (three parts):

A. CHOOSE A TIME AND PLACE.

Do You Both Agree On a Time and Place?

If yes,	If no,
Proceed to Part B.	1. Review steps for Choosing Time and Place, Chapter 4

Example of Choosing Time and Place:
"Is now a good time?" or "How about Saturday afternoon? We can send the kids to the movies."

2. If still no agreement, reaffirm your agreement to negotiate (see Step II) and try again using the reassurance and communications skills outlined in Chapter 3.

B. ESTABLISH GOOD WILL.

Is Good Will Between You Easily Available?

If yes,

State your good will and proceed to Part C.

Example of Expressing Good Will:
"I love you a lot and it's important to me that we enjoy our life together and that's what this negotiation is for."

If no,

1. Use the Establishing Good Will guide, Chapter 4.

2. If good will is not forthcoming, check for held hurt or anger, Chapter 4 and, if necessary, follow the Set Aside

Held Hurt and Anger Guidelines, Chapter 4.

3. If good will is still not forthcoming, let a day or two pass and start over again.

4. If good will is still not forthcoming, see a relationship counselor or therapist.

C. TREASURE.

Are You Both Confident of the Outcome?

If yes,

Proceed to Step IV.

Example of Expressing Reassurance:

"I want to be sure that both of us gets exactly what we want out of this negotiation."

If no,

1. Reassure each other.

2. If reassurance isn't working, follow the Guidelines for Reassurance, Chapters 3 & 4.

Step IV: State Your Wants

Are You Each Clear About Your Own Wants?

If yes,	If no,
Proceed to state your wants.	1. Do the exercise on Clarifying Your Wants, Chapter 5.
_____	

Example of Stating Wants:

Partner A: "I want more time for us to be together: at least one more evening a week. I want to know I'm loved no matter what."

Partner B: "I want to work on my projects, be with you and work out at least twice a week. I want to know I'm loved no matter what."

_____

2. If still unclear, let a day or two pass and review the Problem Inventory, Chapter 2, then with your problem clearly in your mind, redo the exercise on Clarifying Your Wants.

Step IV: State Your Wants (continued):

Are You Both Clear About Your Partner's Wants?

If yes,	If no,
write them out to be certain and proceed to Step V.	1. follow the Guidelines for Sharing Wants in Chapter 5.

Example of Restating Your Partner's Wants:

Partner A: "You want to work on your projects, be with me and work out at least twice a week. You want to know you're loved no matter what."

2. If still unclear, use the Abundance Worksheet in Chapter 6

Partner B: "You want more time for us to be together: at least one more evening a week. You want to know you are loved and appreciated."

3. If still unclear and you seem to be stuck, go back to Step III and establish good will and reassure. Then try again.

Step V: Explore Your Options and Decide (four parts)

A. ESTABLISH OPTIONS.

Are Viable Options Easily Available?

If yes,

choose the option that you can agree upon following the Guidelines for Deciding, Chapter 6, and proceed to Part B.

Example of Restating Your Partner's Wants:

Partner A: "You want to work on your projects, be with me and work out at least twice a week. You want to know you're loved no matter what."

Partner B: "You want more time for us to be together: at least one more evening a week. You want to know you are loved and appreciated."

If no,

1. explore options by expanding boundaries using The Abundance Worksheet, Chapter 6.

2. If no option is suitable, do The Brain storming Exercise, Chapter

3. If no option is suitable, explore wants some more using The Abundance Worksheet, Chapter 6.

4. If no option is suitable, reassure using the Guidelines for Reassurance if necessary, Chapter 4. Then start with expanding boundaries again (A.1 above)

5. If you agree on an option and are unsure of its viability, agree to research using the Guidelines for Doing Research, Chapter 6.

6. If no option is suitable, take a day or two off and come back to it. Review this Negotiation Tree and repeat any parts necessary (e.g., Is this the best

time and place to do this? Do we need to reestablish good will? Is someone needing reassurance?).

7. If no option is suitable, it is possible that the issue being negotiated is a symptom of a deeper problem that can only be resolved with the help of a professional counselor It's OK to get outside help, if necessary.

B. CONFIRM YOUR DECISION.

Each of you state the option(s) selected so that you know you are agreeing to the same option(s).

Do You Each Clearly Agree to the Same Options(s)

If yes, follow the Guidelines for Confirming Your Decision and proceed to Part C.

If no, using your communication skills, analyze your concerns and go back to Part A for more exploration.

Example of Confirming Your Decision:

Partner A: "We'll take a racquetball class at the health club so we can be together and work out too; and our love isn't conditional. We love each other; together or not."

Partner B: "We'll combine being together with working out. We'll take a racquetball class together on Tuesday nights. We reaffirm our unconditional love."

C. WRITING YOUR DECISION (optional).

Follow the Guidelines for Finalizing Your Agreement, Chapter 6 and proceed to Part D.

Example of Your Written Agreement:

1. We will register for a racquetball class on Tuesday nights at the health club beginning in two weeks.

2. We will be together Tuesday nights and weekend nights for sure and at other times as often as we can.

3. I love you whether we are together enough or not. I love you and appreciated you no matter what.

signed _____

signed _____

D. CELEBRATE.

Follow the Guidelines for Celebration, Chapter 6.

As you can see on The Negotiation Tree, there are five main steps to Cooperative Problem Solving:

Step One: Define and Communicate the Problem, in which you learn to clearly define what is bothering you and communicate it to your partner in a way that will make it easy for them to hear, and encourage them to cooperate in solving it.

Step Two: Agree to Negotiate, in which you obtain your partner's agreement to work together cooperatively to solve the problem to your mutual satisfaction.

Step Three: Set the Stage, in which you create a relaxed, uninterrupted atmosphere conducive to working together calmly and effectively.

Step Four: State and Explore Wants, in which both of you discover what you want relative to the problem, and work to communicate your wants to each other, and understand your partner's wants.

Step Five: Explore Your Options and Decide, in which you learn to brainstorm to create new, innovative ideas for solving the problem, until you have selected a mutually satisfactory solution; then confirm your solution to eliminate any possible confusion and celebrate your success.

For each of the five steps The Negotiation Tree will ask you to carry out an action of cooperative problem solving such as define the problem, and then refers to the section and page in the book that explains that step, so, if you don't remember what that step entails, or you get confused or stuck and need help, you can look up the description of that step: that section of the book will tell you, in detail, exactly what you must do to define the problem.

Next, it will ask you a yes or no question, such as "is the problem clear to both of you?" and gives you two options (the possible answers to the question): yes and no. If the answer to the question is yes, you follow the instruction in the yes column, ("If yes, state problem, and proceed to step II"). If no, The Tree will tell you what to do: ("If no, do The Problem Indicator Inventory (Chapter 3) until problem is clear, and try again.").

In this way, The Negotiation Tree will lead you, step by small step, through the negotiation process, and anytime a step doesn't work (you get a no answer) it will direct you to the chapter where you will find the appropriate exercise or guideline that you need at that moment to solve the problem cooperatively.

The Tree points out each step in the procedure in sequence, with instructions and examples of what to do at each step, when to go on to the next step, and when to refer to the exercises and explanations in the book because a step is not complete. The Negotiation Tree is designed as a teacher for beginners and as a trouble shooting aid for more experienced negotiators. In this way, the Negotiation Tree leads you, safely and step by small step, through the entire process.

With the step-by-step methods taught here, whenever you reach an impasse with each other, and feel impossibly stuck or locked in a struggle, you can find solutions for problems that appear to be unsolvable. We have designed The Negotiation Tree and the exercises in such a way that they will guide and encourage you when you feel frustrated, hopeless, or afraid you can't resolve problems.

These processes help you learn to work together rather than struggle with each other over the solutions to problems, disagreements and conflicts, and establish habit patterns that will develop the teamwork of a cooperative happy partnership between you.

Every possibility is covered, and every step is explained in a chapter of the book, which is clearly referenced in the Negotiation Tree. No matter what the difficulty you encounter in trying to solve your problems The Negotiation Tree will guide you to a satisfactory solution every time!

When you have any unsolved problem, unresolved disagreement, or difficult conflict, you can use The Negotiation Tree as a guideline, and it will teach you cooperative problem solving as it guides you through the process.

How to Begin

If you need to solve something right away, and cannot wait, you can begin by following the Negotiation Tree, and allowing it to show you the most appropriate and needed exercises, guidelines, examples, and sections of the book for your situation.

Read the Book First

We strongly recommend reading the book and doing the relevant exercises before using The Negotiation Tree, so that you will have a basic understanding of the terms, guidelines, and skills before you use them for the first time.

Choose a Simple Problem

When you have read the book, done the exercises, and feel ready to try Cooperative problem solving, we recommend that you select a problem that seems simple and straightforward. A small problem that doesn't have an emotional charge and seems easy to resolve will give you a chance to learn the process. Try a problem that you normally just let one person decide without negotiation, such as which movie to see or where to eat, only this time agree not to compromise, and negotiate with the intent of both of you getting exactly what you want, through Cooperative problem solving.

Because The Negotiation Tree helps you focus on creative, new ideas, you may find that you will go out dancing or to a play or concert instead of a movie, or pick up food from two different restaurants and go to a drive in movie, so each of you can have different things at the same time!

By keeping the problem simple the first time, you can have a chance to learn how problem solving works. Problems like "what shall we do this weekend?" or "who does the dishes tomorrow?" are more likely to be successful first-time experiences than emotionally-laden problems (We're not having enough sex) that have been longstanding and frustrating to either one or both of you.

Practice Problem Solving

Run through the process several times over the next few days, practicing with small problems. When you get stuck, use The

Negotiation Tree as your guide to the relevant exercises and instructions. When negotiating small problems gets easy, challenge yourselves by picking a slightly tougher problem to negotiate. If you've picked a problem that is too tough, either break it down into several, simpler problems, or go to a different, easier problem for more practice, (As Suzie and Mike do in the following example) then come back to the tougher problem again.

When Suzie and Mike negotiate about spending money and find that there is not enough money for both to do what they want to do, they could struggle, argue or fight over who gets what they want. Instead, they realize that they have an opportunity to work together if they break their negotiation down further, from who gets to spend the money to negotiating over how to create more money. As they work together to resolve their money problem, they might find hidden resources, alternative and inexpensive ways to have what they want, and that their lack of money is temporary, a minor inconvenience, and begin to plan to create the extra money they need.

Until you get as familiar with the process as Suzie and Mike are, you may occasionally get stuck or confused while experimenting. This is to be expected, and The Negotiation Tree will tell you what to do if this happens.

Having difficulty or getting lost in the problem solving process when you're this new at it just means you are practicing and you have a little more to learn. Negotiating is not difficult or painful, but in the beginning, learning a new skill can feel awkward and clumsy.

Experiment

As you begin to experiment, you'll see the steps are simple and easy to understand, and a little experimentation will convince you that the process works. The only way you can fail at Cooperative problem solving is to quit before you learn all the essential skills this book teaches.

With a little practice, you'll find it soon becomes quite comfortable and easy. The goal of cooperation is to make negotiating a pleasant and successful process. In a relatively short time, it can become second nature to negotiate as a partnership; the success rate you will experience when you try cooperative negotiation will be very rewarding.

It is worth taking the extra time to learn this now, because once you become expert at Cooperative problem solving, it will make problems easy to solve for the rest of your life, and it will give you the confidence to try working together on problems you always thought were impossible to solve. After a few months, you'll be negotiating many aspects of your relationship, until it becomes fully satisfying, easily sustainable, and you both realize you have developed a happy, working partnership.

From their experience of cooperative negotiating, Happy Partners know the effectiveness of working together to solve problems and the good feeling of teamwork that enhances their good will and trust so they face every disagreement, struggle, problem or question with the belief that it can probably be solved in a mutually satisfactory way, and that the only solution that will really work is a cooperative solution, because a competitive, win/lose solution will undermine their partnership.

This new approach to solving problems works precisely because it is so rewarding. When both of you have enough experience at cooperative problem solving to realize that you can't lose, you will approach disagreements, problems and discussions with a new sense of confidence. You will soon see that each problem solving session adds new strength and resilience to your relationship; because it adds to your conviction that together you can work anything out successfully. Once you learn the process, you will consider no problem solved until you both get exactly what you want. You will view each other as helpmates, team partners, who enhance and add to each other's ideas and options. The more problems you solve, the stronger your bond becomes.

If Your Partner Isn't Cooperating

Although ideally you and your partner will use The Negotiation Tree together, you can also use The Negotiation Tree to learn better relating and communicating skills and solve relationship problems by yourself. There may be times when you understand cooperative problem solving, are clear about the benefits, and your partner is suspicious, uninterested, unavailable or unwilling to try.

The idea of negotiating may sound intimidating and scary to your partner until you both try it, and he or she may be hesitant to cooperate at first, but we have provided for that contingency, and the Negotiation Tree (Guidelines for Solving It Yourself) shows you exactly how to take the pressure off your partner and yourself, and make Cooperative Negotiation very inviting to your mate.

One of the unique features of The Negotiation Tree is that it shows you how to be clear about what your problem is, communicate it more effectively to your partner, and persist in a way that increases the possibility of enlisting your partner in Cooperative Negotiation. By reading the book by yourself, even if your partner is uninterested so far, you can still learn Cooperative problem solving and how to make cooperation attractive and inviting to a partner. If your partner resists negotiating, The Negotiation Tree will direct you to the guidelines on "Gentle Persistence" which will give you instructions for maximum effectiveness in inviting him or her to cooperate with you.

If you are reading this book on your own, begin with finding a simple problem, defining it so you understand it, practicing how to state the problem clearly, and try Cooperative problem solving even though your partner doesn't know about it. Announce to your partner that you need some help with something, and then define the problem. Ask if your partner will help you to solve it, and negotiate with you.

As The Negotiation Tree says, if your partner says yes, proceed according to the tree. If you don't, solve the problem for yourself, but announce to your partner what your solution is, and that you're still open to negotiation if your partner is interested. This maximizes your partner's incentive to join in and work together with you. This will show your partner the benefit of getting to be part of the solution, even if they know nothing about cooperative problem solving. (If Suzie keeps putting Mike off when he wants to talk about budgeting money, Mike can decide he's going to get a separate checking account so he can at least control his share of the money, and invite Suzie to discuss it with him if she has a different idea).

If You Are Single

If you are single, and preparing for a future relationship, you can use The Negotiation Tree to help solve your problem by learning to use cooperative problem solving with friends and family. Knowing how to clearly communicate what's important to you, to accurately understand what a prospective partner wants and needs and to be able to work out differences cooperatively will prepare you for the relationship you want, and help you achieve it smoothly and successfully. When you do find the partner you hope for, having these skills will enable both of you to develop a happy partnership from the beginning.

After deciding on a simple beginning problem, copy The Negotiation Tree so you can follow it; and begin with the first step, Define the Problem, which is fully explained in the next chapter.

Chapter Two

Define and Communicate the Problem

The Negotiation Tree begins with a seemingly simple instruction: Define the Problem. This first step in negotiation may seem obvious, but its function is to make sure that you understand the problem thoroughly enough to clearly communicate it in a way your partner can hear and understand.

Many couples' problems remain unsolved because, while one partner believes the problem is obvious and self-evident, the other partner is confused or unclear about what's wrong, or even unaware that there is a problem. Even when both agree there is a problem they often cannot get it clearly defined so that both partners understand it or agree on it Consider the example of Rose and John.

Rose and John

Rose is a housewife in her forties. Her three children are grown, the youngest in high school, and she feels depressed and unhappy. The last twenty-five years of her life were focused on making her home pleasant and caring for her children and husband. It was her full-time job. Now, gradually, her major role has become obsolete. The children are young adults, and don't need her very much, and her husband, John, a lawyer, is away much of the time in his high-powered career. Rose knows she is unhappy, but has trouble understanding why. She tries to talk to John:

Rose: John, I don't know what's wrong, but I feel bad.

John: Gee, I'm sorry to hear that. Why don't you go to the doctor?

Rose: No, it's not that. My health is OK. I just feel listless and tired.

John: Are you getting enough rest? Maybe you're just recovering from the flu you had last month.

Rose: (giving up) Yes, I guess you're right.

John: Get some rest, and you'll feel better. (Ends discussion; goes back to the work he brought home).

Despite John's dismissal, Rose does have a problem, and therefore so does he. John will be profoundly affected if his wife becomes severely depressed or despondent. Neither of them can get clear enough about what's wrong. John tries (more than some spouses might) to be supportive and caring, but he hasn't enough information to go on, and no skills to find out more. Plus, Rose's mood may be scary to him. He dismisses the problem, Rose surrenders to her hopelessness, and no negotiation takes place. Because Rose and John cannot define what the problem is, there is no way they can begin to solve it.

The problem will grow, become more deep-rooted, and create all kinds of little secondary problems:

- Because Rose is depressed, she doesn't do housework or cook, and John becomes angry, or
- Rose feels so miserable, she is easy prey for an affair with a con artist who might use and discard her, leaving her with massive guilt and even more depression, or
- Rose is so depressed, she doesn't respond sexually, so John is tempted to have an affair, or
- Rose uses alcohol, food or shopping to blunt her pain, and creates all the havoc that addictions can engender: emotional, physical, and/or financial.

In this way, a relatively mundane and simple problem which is undefined, and therefore could not be solved, can become a major issue and even the cause for divorce.

Defining the problem helps you pinpoint and clarify exactly what is upsetting or uncomfortable, which it easy to communicate clearly to a partner, thus inviting discussion. Surprisingly, couples often find that defining the problem is all they need to do to solve it, because once both people understand what the trouble is, the solution may become obvious.

For example, if Rose can get clear enough about what her problem is to define it to John, things can go very differently:

Rose: (determined to communicate) John, I feel bad, I have some ideas about why, and I need your help and understanding.

John: Gee, I'm sorry to hear that; I've got a lot of work to do tonight, but I'll help if I can. What's wrong?

Rose: (she's thought a lot about it) I've been very listless and tired, and I've thought about it, and I think I'm sad because I don't feel needed enough anymore.

John: (not getting it) Don't be silly, hon, I need you. I wouldn't know what to do without you.

Rose: (not deterred) Yes, I know you do, but that's not enough to use all my time and talent. My life has changed since the children are grown, and our empty nest has affected me more than you. I need to discuss some possible solutions with you before I get more depressed about it and create a problem for both of us.

John: (hearing, for the first time, that it's important) Wow, it sounds important, Hon, and I do want to talk to you about it, but I have a lot of work tonight. Can we talk about it later?

Rose: (making a mental note to bring up the subject on the weekend) Yes. Now that I know you hear me, I can wait until this weekend to talk. (Rose now knows they can get to the next step, so she ends the discussion, and John goes back to the work he brought home. They'll continue the negotiation process later.)

Because Rose has taken the time to get clear about what her problem is, she is much better able to communicate it to John. She also knows that it's her responsibility to follow up and make sure she and John work together on it. She is determined not to allow him to ignore the severity of the problem or to put her off, and she is prepared to help

33

him understand that, unsolved, this will create problems for him, too.

So this step, Defining the Problem, consists of both the mental exercise of getting clear about what the problem is for you (usually the most difficult part) and a communication exercise, in showing your partner three things:

1) That there is a problem, whether or not your partner is aware of it,

2) What the problem is, in your opinion, and

3) The importance of solving the problem (in other words, how your partner will benefit from cooperatively solving this problem, whether or not he or she realizes it.)

Learning to clearly define the source of dissatisfaction or discomfort that first make you aware of a problem, to communicate it effectively, to invite cooperation, and to recognize when you are being heard are the skills you will learn in this step of The Negotiation Tree.

Barriers to Defining the Problem

Although some problems may be easily defined and communicated (you're angry because your partner isn't doing chores, you don't like the way the two of you interact at parties, you have an investment problem to discuss) you may encounter more difficulty when you attempt defining problems that are more complex or confusing (you have a vague, pervasive unhappiness, you feel neglected or unappreciated, you're not sure how much responsibility each of you should have).

This chapter will help you with those times when you have trouble defining exactly what you need to discuss with your partner. For most people, four common barriers arise, when they attempt to define the problem: 1) Confusion, 2) Rebellion and Compliance, 3) Shoulds, and 4) Secret Expectations.

Through the exercises in the Defining the Problem section you will learn skills to overcome Confusion, Rebellion and Compliance, Shoulds, and Secret Expectations:

- *A Problem Inventory* to help you define and communicate your needs and wants clearly, so both you and your partner can understand the problem, and learning to translate your negative statements (what you don't want) to positive statements (what you want), which overcomes the barrier of confusion.

- *A Compliance and Rebellion* Inventory which will help you recognize and disarm competition, compliance or rebellion when it arises.
- *Creating Permission* which will teach you how to disarm Shoulds, and
- *A Rights and Responsibilities Analysis which* will help you change your Secret Expectations into open agreements.

With these skills, you will be able to successfully define the problem and move on to the next step, the Agreement to Negotiate.

Barrier One: Confusion

Most of us first become aware of a problem because of a vague sense of uneasiness, discomfort, frustration or listlessness. Few of us know, instantly and certainly, exactly what is bothering us, or what to do about it. You may find yourself thinking "If it weren't for (your partner, your job, the weather, etc.) I'd feel better." or even wondering if you're slightly ill (Maybe I'm coming down with something, I've been working too hard, It must be that time of the month, Perhaps I'm tired).

Sorting through this confusion, learning to be responsive to the inner prompting that says a problem exists rather than ignoring it, and taking enough time to achieve clarity about what's bothering you will make a tremendous difference in your problem-solving abilities, at home and elsewhere. Too often, couples create problems on top of problems by being unclear about what the original issue is, or by ignoring discomfort or dissatisfaction until the problem has intensified and grown into overwhelming proportions. The Problem Inventory exercise will teach you how to identify, define and be appropriately aware of potential problems before lack of clarity turns your molehill-sized, everyday problems into mountains.

The Problem Inventory: How to Clear Confusion

It is quite easy to see that Rose is confused when she first tries to define her problem to John. Because she isn't clear about exactly what the problem is, she can't explain it effectively to John, and he, not knowing how important it is, quite nonchalantly brushes the problem (and consequently Rose) off.

Like John, most of us are not eager to have a new problem brought to our awareness in the middle of everything else we have to do. Most of us do not go looking for more problems to solve. So, if the problem is unclear, and doesn't sound important, we are quite relieved to ignore it, and the problem doesn't get solved until it grows into a big, unpleasant issue.

That means you need to learn about how to communicate problems to your partner in such a way that he or she can hear and understand, yet not feel defensive, overwhelmed or hopeless about solving it, thus making it more likely that you will have your partner's help in solving the problem, and, therefore, that the difficulty will get satisfactorily solved.

Defining the problem includes explaining to your partner why solving the problem is good for both of you, because, until your partner understands the gains to be derived from solving it, it won't seem worth the effort, and the problem will seem to be only yours. The better you are at defining it, and making it clear why and how your problem will impact on your partner, the more motivated your partner will be to help you solve it.

If you recognize that a problem exists (that is, you are uncomfortable, unhappy or dissatisfied in some way) but you feel vague or confused about exactly what it is, the following Problem Inventory will help you sort through confusion and understand the problem clearly. By taking the time to list and evaluate the indicators, and create a clear statement of the problem, you can greatly enhance the effectiveness of your communication with your partner, because you'll understand the problem enough to explain it. A clear explanation will motivate your partner to want to solve the problem because the benefit will be understood, and you'll be able to work together cooperatively to solve problems faster and easier, before they become a source of trouble.

Exercise: The Problem Inventory

For this exercise, you'll need a pen and paper, a computer or tablet to write on, some quiet, undisturbed time, and a comfortable place to be alone, to think, and to write. No matter how difficult or longstanding your problem is, The Problem Inventory will show how to analyze your feelings and indicators to better understand the problem, so you can communicate it to your partner.

1. List the problem indicators:

No matter how confused or uncertain you are, you have some reason to believe there's a problem; because you are aware of some feeling (sadness, anger, confusion), physical sensation (tightness in the chest, a tension headache), circumstance (one of you is procrastinating at doing chores or paying the bills), or interaction with your partner (one of you was critical or angry for no apparent reason.) These are your Problem Indicators.

Confusion is usually caused by a number of conflicting or competing ideas and feelings. If you list these Problem Indicators, you can see each one individually, and your confusion will lessen. On your paper, make a heading called Problem Indicators, and write down whatever experience or feeling that first indicated to you that there might be a problem.

For example, Rose's list might read:

- I'm crying a lot
- I feel frustrated
- I feel useless
- There's not enough to do
- I'm eating too much
- Unrealistic fantasy about having another baby

- John seems to be pushing me away.

List everything that seems to indicate a problem even if they seem too obvious to mention: such as a fight between you and your partner, or too silly, such as a dream or a passing thought that seems connected.

The more complex or longstanding the problem is, the more time you will have had to develop and observe indicators, and the longer your list will be. Listing the indicators will also help you to become aware of the less obvious ones because you'll stop ignoring or glossing over them when you give them some thought. Don't rush this step: take enough time, at least ten to fifteen minutes or longer, if you feel very confused. When you finally think your list includes all the important indicators, go to step two.

2. Evaluate your indicators:

Review each indicator on your list. Look for central themes of emotion, things or situations: are your indicators about time, money, power or control, freedom, loss, comfort, sadness, anger, fear, self-criticism, frustration? Several items about crying, depression or loss would indicate a theme of sadness. If several items are about being rushed, no time to play, or wasting time, that's a time theme. Identifying a theme of emotion, things or situations gives you a way to evaluate and understand the hidden meaning of your indicators and organize them into categories, which will make the hidden dynamics of the problem clearer.

Next to each indicator on your list, write the appropriate theme. If you're not sure what the theme for one indicator is, put a question mark (?) next to it, and go on to the others. After you get through the rest of the items, that one may be clearer, and you can write the theme next to the question mark. If not, go back to Step One, and think about it a little more, and see if you can make the theme come clear. If it's still not clear, put it aside until after you've done Step Three, and concentrate on the items you feel clear about.

Here's what Rose's list looked like after this step:

- I'm crying a lot (loss)

- I feel frustrated (?) [on second pass] (time, loss, self-criticism)
- I feel useless (self-criticism)
- There's not enough to do (time)
- I'm eating too much (self-criticism, comfort)
- Unrealistic fantasy about having another baby (loss)
- John seems to be pushing me away (loss)

Rose's list is about time (too much on her hands), loss (children are not around much anymore, John ignoring her, she cries) and self-criticism (she feels useless, eats too much) from which she needs to comfort herself (eating).

3. Put the themes into a sentence:

Below your indicator list, write the themes you found. Rose's list would be "time, loss, and self-criticism." Using these themes, compose a sentence or two that describes the problem. After thinking a while, Rose wrote "I'm experiencing loss, because my children are gone and I have time on my hands. Now that I'm not taking care of them anymore I criticize myself a lot, and I feel worthless." When you have completed your sentence, go on to the next step.

If you have a lot of trouble identifying themes and creating a sentence, put this exercise aside, and do the exercises that follow in this chapter. As you explore your own relationship to rebellion and compliance, shoulds, and secret expectations, you'll discover what blocks prevent you from clarifying the problem. Then return to finish this exercise.

4. Review for clarity:

Now that you have clarified your confusion, and have a description of the problem that you understand the next step is to make sure it will be clear and not confusing to your partner. Review your descriptive sentence to see whether it's clear enough to be understandable to your partner.

You can pretend your partner is sitting opposite you and practice explaining the problem to him or her. Your purpose is simply to define the problem, and not to express your feelings. if you let frustration or resentment creep in, and phrase the problem in terms of blaming someone (even yourself), your partner will probably react with defensiveness and confusion, and you won't be able to move ahead in your negotiation.

Keep in mind that you're describing the problem as you experience it. State it in terms of yourself: For example, Rose will be more likely to be heard if she says "I feel useless and not very important now that the children are grown." than if she says "The children never call, and you're neglecting me", because John can be more sympathetic and less defensive if he doesn't feel criticized or attacked. (If you now clearly understand what your problem is, but you cannot express it without resentment or fear, read the next section, Compliance and Rebellion.)

Review and refine your statement of the problem until you are ready to communicate it positively to your partner, and you feel quite sure your partner will be able to understand it.

5. Learn from your experience:

This final step will help you become more sensitive to the signals that tell you a problem exists, which will make recognizing and defining the problem easier as time goes on. Review what you've learned about your confusion while you were doing the previous steps of this exercise, to analyze what your indicators are. For example, a tense feeling in the pit of your stomach, a headache, exhaustion, or depression might be an Indicator that shows up whenever you have a problem, and by becoming sensitive to these recurring signs, you can become aware of unsolved problems much sooner. As you do this exercise several times for different problems, you will begin to see a pattern to the indicators.

For example, Rose often eats too much when she is unhappy but has not yet defined the problem. By becoming aware of this indicator, whenever she notices she's overeating, she can immediately take the time to define her problem, stop the overeating, and handle the problem while it's still small and manageable.

Your recurring Indicators may include butterflies in your stomach, sleep disturbances or dreams, or irritability. Once you know these are just problem indicators they will not be as upsetting, and as you work on defining the problem, those indicators will subside. When you've done this exercise many times, it will become quite easy to analyze your problem indicators and define the problem quickly, without formally writing them down.

Shoulds

We all have rules for being who we are, and living as we do: things we should or should not do, such as the Ten Commandments, rules of etiquette; and standards that define behavior as generous or selfish. Some of these rules are well-thought out, effective guidelines learned from our life experience; and others are unconscious prejudices and mistaken beliefs we acquired early and have never examined or changed.

We all grow up with ideas of how we should be in relationships, proper roles for gender, and how husbands, wives and unmarried people must act. If these rules are too rigid, they can become limiting, stressful, awkward or hampering, and interfere with happiness and success.

Believing you should behave a certain way can be a barrier to Defining the Problem. When your needs, desires, or circumstances challenge or contradict an inner rule, you feel confused and guilty; which may cause you to suppress or ignore what you really want, and make you unable to create a truly satisfying life for yourself.

Here you will learn about cultural rules and family rules for being who you are, exercises to make these rules more adaptable to your actual life by turning your shoulds into permissions. The exercises help you explore the unconscious rules that may be running your relationship, and achieve the freedom of choice you need to create a mutually satisfying partnership.

Shoulds: Rules, Customs and Traditions

Shoulds are arbitrary rules for relating that do not consider your individual needs or practical concerns; they can be a major barrier to clearly understanding and defining your problem. If you are feeling unhappy, uncomfortable or frustrated in your relationship, and you are having trouble defining the problem, you may be in conflict with or unaware of your own internal rules for relationship. For example, if Rose believes she should be happy and fulfilled as a housewife, she'll have trouble admitting or understanding that she is unhappy because her life lacks meaning.

Because we learn the rules for living in our family as small children, without the ability to judge or evaluate what we are taught, we don't examine them for effectiveness, functionality and health. Instead, they are learned by inference, example, and (often painful) experience. You aren't directly told how you must be in your relationship, but through approval, disapproval and example you learn what is expected of you. These ideas of the right thing to do are often mistaken or even destructive and dysfunctional.

The three most common types of rules are:

Traditional Rules:

These are social customs everyone knows and they often seem natural, but when you try to follow them, they don't always work.

Traditional rules are changing in today's society, but people still fight to keep the old rules. When you think about them you use words like acceptable, right, proper and normal. They are the unspoken rules most people seem to follow, and belittle others for not following.

Examples of traditional rules are:

- Women do housework and childcare,
- Men earn the money.
- Women wait to be asked.
- Men take the lead.

- Don't talk openly and honestly about emotions, sex, or money.
- Lying or denying is better than upsetting people.

Gender Stereotypes

These define our roles as men and women; that men should behave in one way and women in another and those ways may not be compatible with individual personalities and desires. The rules for your own gender affect your behavior, and those for the other gender affect your choice of a partner, or, if you are in a same-sex relationship, they may affect the roles you play.

For example:

- Men aren't emotional.
- Women are too emotional
- A single man avoids commitment, a single woman wants marriage.
- A man is responsible in the world; a woman is responsible in the home.
- A marriage is between a man and a woman
- Men and women wear different clothing
- Women can't do the same jobs as men or earn the same money.

Family Traditions:

Families have their own unwritten rules. You learn most of them from watching what adults did:

- Daddy (therefore all men) yells when there's a problem,
- Mommy (therefore all women) suffers silently.
- It's grown-up and sexy to smoke (drink, drive fast).
- Problems are never talked about, there's just a lot of tension in the air.
- The family is more important than the individual in it.

- Our family spends more than it has

If Rose was brought up to believe that women are supposed to be fully satisfied within the home, and are not supposed to make waves, she could have a lot of trouble even realizing why she was unhappy, and even more difficulty defining the problem so that John could understand. As long as Rose was content at home, the rule was not a problem; but when circumstances changed, Rose was trapped by complying with a rule that no longer fit.

When you grow up with one set of ideas, and find a partner whose family and experience was different; conflict is almost guaranteed, because each of you will feel very strongly that the other is not doing what should be done.

If Joe's mother had been home with him all the time when he was a child, and Carol's mother worked, Joe and Carol will most likely have conflicting ideas (built on their different childhood experiences) about the woman's role in the relationship. While Joe and Carol might both enjoy (or need) the money Carol's career generates, when she can't get home from work before Joe she may be shocked and confused by how resentful or unreasonably angry he is.

Like Carol and Joe, most people are unaware of the shoulds that describe how we are supposed to be in a relationship. Social rules can be useful, because they help bring order to our lives and guide us in dealing comfortably with strangers, business associates and social contacts; but they often cause problems in intimate relationships. As we become intimate and get to know each other's more private selves; we interact on an emotional, no longer social level. To make intimacy work, we must deal with each other as caring individuals.

Becoming aware of your traditional, social and family rules makes it possible for you to clearly understand the difference between what you should do, and what will be effective and satisfying.

For example, Carol believes that, as a woman, she must take care of Joe and his needs before she takes care of herself, so she doesn't understand she is overburdened, and her depression and anxiety are a result of her stress. Joe, too, believes that as a man, he shouldn't be concerned about his emotional needs or his own comfort and care. These rules keep them frustrated, unhappy, and unsatisfied with the relationship and stuck in roles that aren't working.

You let rules stop you from defining the problem when you:

- Believe you shouldn't have the problem (Rose may be intelligent and motivated to go to school, but her shoulds say she should be content as a housewife).

- Feel you can't say what you want (As a child, Joe learned not to complain or speak up when he was unhappy and today it prevents him from letting Carol know what he wants).

- Believe you can't make a choice (Carol and Joe could use the extra money, but Joe's belief that women stay home makes him resist Carol's working, even though she wants to).

- Deny some of your natural abilities and aspirations (John would like to take guitar lessons, but his shoulds say that's too frivolous, so he says he's too busy with work).

- Have different rules about how to communicate (Dale learned that whoever yelled loudest won the argument, Don learned not to talk about it at all, so Dale yells, Don clams up, and they never Define the Problem).

Getting past these subconscious rules clears up confusion, reluctance and feeling stuck. Whenever you feel stuck, you can search for the rule that is restricting you, and in its place create permission. This will make it easier to define a problem by giving you the freedom to act according to what is actually needed, rather than be limited by rules that may not apply.

Even when you both agree on some rules, rigid adherence them doesn't work in the long run, because it is boring and tiring and doesn't always fit your changing circumstances. Having permission to customize your relationship in whatever way works is much more realistic and sustainable. Creating permission gives you the flexibility to be able to make your rules more flexible when they conflict, communicate more openly and honestly about what's wrong, and therefore, to define problems readily.

Exercise: Creating Permission

Re-read your problem indicator list from the problem inventory exercise; and you'll discover the indicators are connected to cultural, family, traditional and personal rules which prevent you from seeing the problem clearly. Next to the problem indicators, list the rules which are creating the blockage.

Once you realize how traditional, gender and family rules for behavior have been preventing you from defining the problem, and you know what some of these rules are, the next step is to give yourself permission to change should into could. You can easily create permission to follow, alter or ignore traditional, family and gender rules rule when you think "I could" instead. On your list, each rule that causes problems in your relationship and change it into permission or a choice.

For example, one of Rose's rules was "women are supposed to be fully satisfied within the home". She rewrote that rule: "As a woman, I could choose to work, go to school, or be a housewife, depending on what I want, and what our needs are."

Competition, Rebellion and Compliance

Even after you have done the problem inventory, and you feel clear about what your problem is, you may find you still have some reluctance to approach your partner with the problem, or some difficulty articulating it calmly. If you feel like attacking or blaming your partner or fighting about the issue, or you're reluctant or afraid to bring the problem to your partner, you are probably experiencing either Rebellion or Compliance. You get locked in a struggle about who has the power (or is in charge) in the relationship.

Saying what you want is a risk if you're afraid of hurting your partner or being disappointed or deprived, or if you feel it's self-centered, greedy, or impolite to ask for what you want. It can be scary to say what you want or you're unhappy about. Or, you may feel that a want is a challenge and when you try to listen and accept what your partner is saying you may automatically jump to the defense, and try to win. When you believe someone wins and someone loses, or that someone has to be right and one wrong, you'll try to win or defend yourself. Under this belief system, your only choice is to give in (comply) or compete (rebel.)

On the other hand, if you give in and let your partner win, your relationship will seem smooth for a while, but your anger will creep out in subtle, passive/aggressive ways (losing sexual desire, being depressed and miserable, getting sick) or in periodic explosions over insignificant issues. Consequently, both you and your partner will feel dissatisfied, frustrated, unequal, resentful, and unhappy.

If Rose accepted that all problems result in someone winning and the other person losing, she might have assumed that John would win, and everything would have to stay as it was, and never have brought the problem up until she was so upset, depressed or desperate that she had a meltdown. Or, she might have decided that to win, she would have to rebel: get angry and make demands of John, who would then probably react to her attitude and struggle against her. In the first example, Rose did bring the problem up, but gave up easily and complied with what she thought he wanted, feeling she had lost.

Many rules and restrictions are self-imposed, and have little to do with your partner attempting to control or coerce you. Your partner may not intend to be controlling or passive, and you may not either. Bickering is based on confusion and old habit patterns and can usually be solved by learning to negotiate as equals. The Compliance and Rebellion inventory teaches you to identify the source of your struggles, so you can get past this barrier to negotiating and cooperating.

If you have a history of being in dysfunctional, codependent, or abusive relationships or are a survivor of childhood abuse, this issue of compliance or rebellion will be a very big one for you, and you might want to seek counseling to help you learn to protect yourself and maintain your equality.

Exercise: Compliance and Rebellion Inventory

You and your partner can do this exercise separately. Do not share or discuss your answers until you are instructed to do so.

The quiz:

Answer the following questions by filling in the blanks with "always", "sometimes" or "never".

- When something needs to be done around the house, I_____initiate the necessary action.
- I am___in charge of how we spend money.
- I_____feel angry when I am left out of decisions.
- I_____find it harder to do something if my partner wants me to.
- I will___fight to win an argument even if I know I'm wrong.
- I_____feel like a parent, the boss, or otherwise in charge.
- My partner___feels like an extra burden or responsibility for me.
- I_____resist asking for help, or being taken care of.
- I am___sure that my partner can't manage things as well as I can.
- When household chores need doing, I double check to see if my partner is doing what he or she is supposed to.

Rate your answers as follows: 1 point for each always, 2 for each sometimes, and 3 for each never. Now add up your score and compare it to the following analysis:

10-15 points:

You won't have a difficult time defining the problem or understanding what it is, because you are used to being in charge; knowing what's wrong, and what to do about it. The problem may be that you will also try to define everyone else's problems for them. You may also have trouble communicating a problem to your partner, or getting his or her cooperation, because you have a tendency to tell your partner what the solution should be, (which causes your partner to rebel and argue, or comply and insincerely agree, clam up or not participate) rather than negotiating and creating the solution with your partner as a teammate. In the following discussion, make an extra effort to listen to your partner's feelings, ideas and opinions, rather than be so focused on your own ideas and solutions.

16-25 points:

You feel quite equal to your partner, are more willing to negotiate, and probably pretty evenly balanced between being compliant and rebellious. You value teamwork and mutual agreement. Defining the problem is fairly easy for you, because you are used to thinking for yourself, and you will probably be able to communicate it well enough for your partner to understand. You will probably enjoy the following discussion, and it will help you build even more teamwork, because you will keep an even balance between listening to your partner, and sharing your own thoughts.

26-30 points:

Even when you have used the problem inventory to help you, you will probably have some trouble defining the problem, because you will have trouble feeling your needs are important enough to bring the problem up to your partner. But, if you allow the problem to go un-negotiated, you will eventually resent the situation and feel unsatisfied and trapped. In the discussion section, concentrate on speaking up for yourself and invite your partner to help you be more assertive about what you want. If you are afraid your partner will mistreat you if you speak up, get some professional help by calling a local domestic violence hotline.

The discussion:

With your partner or a good friend, discuss the above quiz as follows:

1. Compare Answers:

Reread each of the ten questions in the quiz, compare your answers, and each of you take two minutes or less to explain why you answered always, sometimes or never to that particular question. This will help you better understand the ways you rebel or comply, and your reasons for it, which will help you be aware of and correct the behavior as you learn to problem solve as equals.

2. Compare Scores:

Compare your total scores, read the appropriate score interpretation paragraphs, and discuss whether you think the evaluation is appropriate for yourself and your partner. If your opinion of your own attitudes of compliance and rebellion differ from what the interpretation says, tell why you think it's different. If your opinion is that the evaluation is accurate, tell why.

Now do the same for each other's evaluation. This will also help you understand and be more aware of rebelling and complying, so you can begin to interact more as an equal with your partner, to improve your communication and problem solving.

3. Consider Changes:

Discuss how your power roles (feeling like parent or child) and patterns of compliance (giving in to or placating your partner) and rebellion (blaming, arguing or fighting back) or hinder your problem-solving and communication, and how it prevents you from clearly Defining the Problem and communicating it to your partner. Talk about how you have fought back, complied or given up in other situations and previous relationships, including your childhood. Also discuss situations in which you have discussed a problem as an equally powerful person, and how that helped you work together. Finish the discussion by recapping how your compliant or rebellious attitudes have created problems in the past, and how you can change your behavior (by saying what you want, not agreeing when you don't want to, calmly giving your different opinion instead of blaming or fighting) so you can solve problems more as equals in the future.

Now that you have tallied your scores, and reviewed or discussed your answers, you have a clearer idea of how much you comply or rebel in your relationship. You may be quite surprised to find out how restricted you feel, and that both you and your partner feel restricted in similar or different ways. Knowing how these restrictions have hindered your problem solving in the past will motivate you to change your old habits of rebellion or compliance and strive to become more equal partners, by learning cooperative negotiation.

Secret Expectations

You may have developed the ability to guess pretty accurately what the people around you want and need from you; because it is often considerate, gracious or polite to anticipate someone's desires. However, in an intimate relationship, things work differently. When you make guesses about what your partner wants and needs, and your partner, in return, makes guesses about you, it is very easy to misinterpret each other's signals; and believe you have a clear understanding of each other without realizing that your interpretations are different. It's also common to feel that because you love each other, you understand each other. It's OK when it works, but when your unconscious rules are combined with uncommunicated expectations, the resulting confusion and chaos makes it very difficult to think clearly enough to define or understand problems enough to communicate or negotiate.

Secret expectations are expectations one person has and assumes the other person understands or knows without ever confirming them verbally. The one who has the Secret Expectation may not even realize how important or significant it is because it's never been discussed or thought about. These expectations get in the way of defining the problem because they keep the problems hidden.

Secret expectations form quite easily, because most of us make assumptions about the future from what has happened before. If Iris and Jan meet on a Wednesday, and then the next week Jan calls and asks Iris out for Wednesday night, and the following week it happens again, when the fourth week arrives, and Jan doesn't call, what will Iris think? She'll most likely be upset, because she thought they were going out every Wednesday. What Iris doesn't know, because it wasn't mentioned, is that Jan has a late business meeting every fourth Wednesday night; and Jan doesn't realize that Iris has a secret expectation that Wednesday is their night out.

Iris' expectation that Jan would call has led to her believe that something is wrong, that Jan may have stopped wanting to see her, because she doesn't know the facts. Iris will be hurt, disappointed and possibly upset, and she and Jan may even have an argument over it.

Secret expectations can get even more emotionally loaded when they are connected to old rules left over from childhood. Joe expects Carol to make dinner at 6:00 every night, because that's what his mother always did. If, in addition, he (probably without being aware of it) believes making dinner on time means Carol loves him (and doesn't care about him if dinner is not ready) then Joe's got a secret expectation. If Carol doesn't know about Joe's expectation, and he doesn't realize that Carol doesn't think dinner on time is so important, a relationship problem is brewing and will catch them by surprise. Things can get even more complicated if Joe thinks Carol's supposed to put dinner on at 6 to show she loves him, and she thinks she's supposed to iron his shirts to show love. Carol may be working very hard at ironing shirts to let Joe know he's loved, and he might be getting angrier and angrier because dinner is late.

Sooner or later, someone's expectations will not be fulfilled, because one of you guessed wrong; and hurt feelings, upsets, and even rage can result. When you feel very confused or upset, or you are not sure why you're fighting, you and your partner have probably developed a Secret Expectation, or unconscious set of rules. It's one of the major reasons problems between couples do not get solved. When your Secret Expectations are no longer secret, the source of many mysterious and confusing upsets in your relationship will be astoundingly clear, and once discussed and understood, it will no longer trouble you.

Don and Dale

For example, Don and Dale, a committed thirtysomething gay couple, think they have a clear agreement about housework. Don thinks his job is taking out the trash, and Dale washes the dishes. But Dale may think he is supposed to wash the dishes while Don waters the plants. Although most of the time everything gets done, for a couple of busy weeks Don doesn't water the plants, assuming Dale will do it. When the plants begin to drop their leaves, Dale accuses Don of "not doing his share around the house". Don, who's been faithfully taking out the trash even though he was busy, is highly insulted and feels unjustly accused.

A secret expectation exists when you make guesses about what your partner wants, and force your partner to guess, by not being open about what you want. Secret expectations are secret because no one ever states out loud "I want you to ..." or asks, "What do you want?" or "would you like me to ...?" In short, no one clearly defines the problem.

If Carol doesn't have dinner ready at 6:00 when Joe gets home, but leaves a note (on his freshly ironed shirts!) that she went to her mother's for dinner, and there's a frozen dinner in the freezer, he may be very upset. Instead of asking what happened, Joe overreacts to the surprise, throws a fit and threatens to divorce her, and Carol is completely mystified, confused and feels unjustly accused of not loving him, because she can only see that he's overreacting to missing dinner.

Long-standing resentment is another telltale sign of hidden expectations. When hidden expectations are not met, resentment will slowly build up, sometimes until it is released in a rage. For example, Dale might not say anything when the plants are not watered and he has to water them, but the more it happens, Dale will get angrier and angrier, until one day he explodes.

The confusion, repeated arguments and explosive interaction caused by secret expectations can be a block to defining the problem, and detrimental to a sustainable, satisfying relationship.

Changing your secret expectations into open agreements disarms them and eliminates the resentment and arguments they cause, while making it much easier to clearly define problems when they come up. Once the secret is out, and you realize expectations exist, it can be quite simple to make an open agreement.

The following exercise will help you become aware when secret expectations are operating, and how to bring them into the open, so you can clearly define and renegotiate them into clear, effective, open agreements.

Exercise: Discovering Secret Expectations

The indicator that secret expectations have been breached is any reaction that is out of proportion to what really happened such as: outrage, irritation, frustration, or resentment. When there's an overreaction (as when Joe blows up because Carol isn't home to fix dinner) you can discover the expectations and backtrack to discover what secret expectations are at work.

Exercise: Secret Expectations in Past Relationships:

1. Review trouble spots:

Mentally review your past relationships for times when a former partner got extremely angry, hurt, afraid, or upset about something you did or didn't do. Write a brief (one or two sentence) description of what happened. Carol wrote: "Joe got unreasonably angry when I wasn't home to make dinner, even though I ironed his shirts, and told him where I was."

2. Review your behavior:

Review your own behavior in those relationships. Were there times when you got upset, angry, frustrated or disappointed out of proportion to what your partner did or didn't do? Write a brief description: "I got very angry when Joe didn't appreciate my ironing enough. I steamed about it for days."

3. Imagine hidden expectations:

Look at these two lists, and try to imagine what the hidden expectations were when the overreactions happened: "Joe must have expected that I would always be home to make dinner, and I must have expected that he would appreciate my ironing his shirts enough to not mind getting his own dinner."

4. Create permissions:

Turn your expectations into permission, by putting could or can in place of should. "I can let Joe know I love him in other ways than by making dinner and ironing shirts. We can talk about what our responsibilities are in the relationship."

Using the above information, discuss your secret expectations with your partner. Discover secret expectations whenever they exist by becoming aware of resentment and overreactions as they happen. Talk about the warning signs you see in yourself and in your partner, the kinds of secret agreements you have had in the past, and what you can do to correct them. When you detect a secret expectation, turn the expectations into permission, and work out a solution together, using problem solving if necessary. Discuss how to bring up the subject in a way that can be heard when either of you believes that your partner is harboring a secret expectation.

Secret expectations often arise when partners don't openly discuss the rights and responsibilities each one has in the relationship. Acknowledging these rights and responsibilities, and agreeing on them makes defining the problem easier, because it helps eliminate secret expectations and the resulting confusion.

Rights and Responsibilities

As partners, you have rights in your relationship and along with these rights come certain responsibilities. For example, both partners have a right to have reasonable sexual needs met, and a responsibility to keep a positive emotional atmosphere that's conducive to lovemaking, and you have a right to be clearly communicated with (and listened to), and a responsibility to do your share of the communicating (and listening).

But different ideas about each partner's rights and responsibilities can be a barrier to Defining the Problem: If you have not determined your different rights and responsibilities neither of you will feel you have the right to ask for what you want; and you will not be able to communicate your dissatisfaction to your partner. Couples often make the mistake of assuming they know what their individual rights and responsibilities are, which leads to having secret, rather than open agreements. Learning to be aware of, and communicate, your mutual rights and responsibilities helps you create open agreements, and clearly define any problems that arise.

As an intimate partner, you have a responsibility to assume an equal share of the normal financial, maintenance and social obligations of life, because Happy Partners (as we discussed in Chapter One) are equal partners. That doesn't mean you have to keep score and always contribute equally, but that your agreement must feel mutual.

In addition, you both have a responsibility to keep your relationship sustainable: that is, to take care of yourself, to ask for help when you need it, and to cooperate with your partner as much as you can without resenting, being deprived or feeling damaged by what's requested of you.

Happy Partners rights include:

- Being able to ask for what you want (and find another solution if the answer is no),
- Saying no to your partner, in order to take care of yourself,
- Doing what you need to do to be happy, healthy and satisfied, and
- Cooperating with your partner in order to create a relationship that you both enjoy.

The following exercise will help you analyze the responsibilities in your relationship, and discover your mutual rights. Clarifying your rights and responsibilities will help you know whether you're exercising your rights and meeting your responsibilities effectively. You can then define and express problems more clearly, recognize your right to be satisfied in each situation, and understand your partner's point of view.

Exercise: Rights and Responsibilities Analysis

You can do this exercise alone or with a partner. If you do not have a current partner, or your partner is not participating, just fill out the "partner" columns as you would think your ideal (or current) partner would fill them out. If you're doing the exercise together, do the columns first alone, and do not share your answers until instructed to do so in the discussion section, so that you won't influence each other's answers.

1. Create columns:

Divide a piece of paper in half, lengthwise, by either folding it or drawing a vertical line down the middle, or set up columns in a computer page. Head one side of the paper "me" and the other "my partner". Under each name, put two column headings: "Rights" and "Responsibilities".

Your page should look like this:

Me	My Partner
Rights Responsibilities	Rights Responsibilities

2. Fill in the column headed Me first:

Under rights, list all the things you see as your rights as a human being, and your rights in the relationship. Reviewing the Rights and Responsibilities Exercise will give you a picture of the rights and responsibilities involved in your daily activities, and help you be more specific. For example, your rights might include the right to privacy, the right to feel what I feel, the right to work when and where I want to, to decide how the money I earn is spent, to go out alone with my friends, the right to ask for what I want and "the right to be heard by my partner". Take your time and get at least ten rights listed.

2. List your responsibilities:

Still working in the Me column, list what you see as your responsibilities. Include chores and work responsibilities as well as emotional responsibilities.

For example, you might say, "the responsibility to do the laundry", "responsibility to listen to my partner", "responsibility to earn enough money", "responsibility to keep peace", "responsibility to keep myself healthy", "responsibility to earn the family's living" "responsibility to say what I want". It's helpful to put related things in both columns, like "the right to be listened to", and "the responsibility to be a good listener".

3. List your partner's rights and responsibilities:

Go to the columns marked my partner, and repeat steps two and three for your partner's rights and responsibilities as you understand them. For example, your partner may want the right to have separate friends, and the responsibility to keep you informed about activities and keep commitments made with you.

4. Evaluate your own list:

Now, compare your columns. Does it look balanced and fair to you? For example, do your rights outweigh your responsibilities or vice versa? If not, go back and add rights to balance each responsibility or vice versa. Do your partner's rights and responsibilities seem about equal to yours? If not, go back and add rights to balance each responsibility or vice versa. Keep adding to your lists, making adjustments until you feel your rights and responsibilities and your partners are approximately equal. Ideally your rights and responsibilities and your partner's will feel mutually satisfying and reasonable to both of you.

5. Discussion:

With your partner, (or having a friend play the role of partner), compare the lists of rights and responsibilities. Make this an opportunity to increase your understanding of each other and your beliefs about the rights and responsibilities in your relationship, by asking questions about differences you have come up with, acknowledging each other's good ideas, and comparing these lists to the actual rights and responsibilities you have in your current relationship. If you find that some of the things on your list are not present in your current relationship, discuss how adopting those rights and responsibilities would change things between you.

6. Create a mutual list:

After your discussion, create a new list with the rights and responsibilities of each partner that you can both agree on. If you find yourselves struggling about a specific right or responsibility, use that as an example for practicing Cooperative Negotiation.

Getting clear about your rights and responsibilities in the relationship will give you the confidence to see that you do have rights, including the right to define and speak up about problems. You will also have a clearer agreement about your mutual rights, and the reassurance that each of you recognizes your responsibilities.

Defining the Problem

Now that you've learned how to overcome the barriers of confusion, rules, rebellion, and compliance and secret expectations that may arise when you attempt to define and communicate a problem to your partner, defining the problem will be quite easy for you to do. As stated in the beginning of this chapter, there are three things to communicate in defining the problem:

1. A problem exists:

The problem inventory will help you resolve any confusion you have and make you clearly aware that there really is a problem to be solved.

The Compliance and Rebellion Inventory and the Rights and Responsibilities Analysis can also be useful in reassuring you that you have a right to ask for help with your problem, and to strengthen your resolve to ask for the cooperation you want. By doing these exercises whenever you feel confused, you can learn to be more confident in your knowledge that a problem exists, just as Rose learned to in the example at the beginning of this chapter.

2. What the problem is:

The final steps of the Problem Inventory are designed to help you become clear about what the problem is. If you still have some doubts or confusion about whether you should feel the way you feel about the issue, re-read the section on Shoulds and Creating Permission, and use the Discovering Secret Expectation exercise to break free from old stereotypes and assumptions that prevent you from seeing it clearly.

3. Why both of you benefit from cooperating:

In order to make your problem clear to your partner, you may need to explain (as Rose did), that if the problem goes unsolved, it will soon be a problem for your mate, too. The Rights and Responsibilities Inventory, Compliance and Rebellion Inventory, Creating Permission, Discovering Secret Expectations, and Problem Inventory, added to the information you already have about why equal partners have more satisfying relationships, will help both you and your partner understand how both of you will benefit from cooperatively solving a problem, even though one or both of you have been unaware that the problem existed until now.

Once you have defined the problem, and communicated it clearly to your partner, you are ready to move on to the next step in The Negotiation Tree: Agree to Negotiate

Chapter Three

Agree To Negotiate

You have identified and clarified the problem, so you are now ready to engage your partner to find a cooperative solution for it and agree to negotiate. No problem can be solved unless you agree to negotiate a solution.

If you attempt to discuss something and wind up competing, fighting, arguing, sacrificing, martyring, feeling manipulated or exploited, giving in to keep the peace or otherwise getting nowhere, you are probably trying to work on the problem without a clear, mutually understood agreement to work together. Your partner can so easily feel ambushed or think that you are complaining, criticizing or just ventilating.

These guidelines have been proven to help you and your partner cooperate rather than compete; and to avoid struggling and fighting. Agreeing to negotiate means you have a spoken contract that each of you will give your best effort and attention to working together to resolve the problem to your mutual satisfaction. Agreeing minimizes competition and struggling and encourages cooperation between you because it establishes the following important criteria for problem solving:

- It establishes that you are Problem-Solving and not discussing, arguing, commiserating or anything else.
- It makes clear your mutual commitment to work together to

solve the problem.

- It will keep you both participating in the process of negotiating.
- It helps you focus your attention on the task of solving the problem.

Michelle and Lou

Michelle, 24, and Lou, 35 struggle over who has the power in their relationship:

Michelle: Lou, you treat me like I'm a little girl all the time and that's getting to be a serious problem for me.

Lou: Well, you act like a little girl. You act so helpless about doing things around the house and about money. What do you expect me to do?

Michelle: There are some things that are easier for you, but that doesn't make me your little girl! There are also some things I'm really good at and you still treat me as if I'm incompetent and unworthy of respect.

Lou: What are you complaining about? I pay the rent and I pay for everything when we go out! You want to start paying half of everything?

Michelle: Maybe I do.

Lou: Hah! That'll be the day.

Because Michelle never mentioned that she would like to solve a problem, Lou interpreted her complaint as an attack, responded defensively and they never got beyond arguing. Michelle's problem of feeling patronized and demeaned is still unsolved (and effectively uncommunicated to Lou), and though Lou may feel that he won, Michelle's frustration and anger from the argument means she won't be interested in the intimacy he wants.

If Michelle had defined the problem and asked for an Agreement to Negotiate, Lou might have felt consulted instead of attacked and therefore been less likely to get defensive, and more open to hear what she was saying.

Arguments can also happen even when one partner clearly offers to negotiate, but the other partner has not clearly agreed to join in. Here Michelle clearly wants to negotiate, and so does Lou, but he is still defensive:

Michelle: (stating problem, taking responsibility for her part, but vague) Lou, I'm getting more and more uncomfortable about how you treat me. My behavior and attitude probably has something to do with it, but I don't know what. Can we talk about this and see if we can solve it?

Lou: I don't like it either. (not a clear agreement)

Michelle: (begins restating problem without a clear agreement) When you tell people that I don't know something or I can't do something, I feel incompetent and uncomfortable. If you would give me credit for knowing what I know and doing what I'm good at, I would feel a lot better.

Lou: (defensive, not trying to cooperate) Well, why don't you talk back? Why don't you stand up for yourself?

Michelle: (beginning to argue) I don't know. It just seems futile, I guess.

Lou: Well, there you are! You just give up! I wish you'd grow up!

Michelle stated her problem and asked to negotiate. Then she proceeded to discuss the problem as if she had gotten an agreement when, in fact, Lou had not agreed to negotiate. That left Lou free to avoid negotiation by criticizing her. Both of you must understand you're working together to solve a problem. Here we'll show you how so you don't wind up struggling.

You'll learn to overcome the barriers to agreeing to negotiate, which will make the remaining steps of The Negotiation Tree easier and speed you on your way toward a truly happy partnership. You can see the change in Lou's response when Michelle uses what she learned about defining the problem, and gets Lou's agreement before negotiating:

Michelle: (clearly defining problem, and taking responsibility for her part) Lou, I have a problem I'd like your help with. I often feel like you're the one in charge and I'm your little girl. I know both of us contribute to that interaction, and I'd like your help in solving that problem. We're both missing out if we can't be our full selves with each other and act as partners. I think you'd get a lot more of what you want if we worked together as equal adults, and I'd like to see the playful little boy side of you once in a while.

Lou: And I'm tired of being grown-up all the time. Let's see if we can negotiate this.

Michelle: OK. (Agreement established)

Now that Lou and Michelle both understand the problem and have clearly agreed to negotiate it, they will both be equally committed to solving the problem, as is the likelihood that they will successfully reach a mutually satisfactory agreement. You don't need to ask for an agreement as formally Michelle did; but you both need to agree.

Fred and Naomi and **Don and Dale** are a little more casual, but just as clear:

Fred: Naomi, I'm really unhappy about our sex life and you seem to be unhappy lately, too. Let's sit down and see if we can sort this out together.

Naomi: Yeah, I'd like to do that.

Don: I'm going to start riding my bike to work on Thursdays so I can save time getting to night class.

Dale: Don, I think that's dangerous and I'd worry about you. Can we talk it over and see if there's a better solution?

Don: OK, I don't want you to worry.

Once you and your partner have some success in cooperative problem solving, agreeing to negotiate is quick, simple and usually easy.

But you may feel resistance if:

- You are not familiar with cooperating.
- You and your partner have a history of struggling,
- You come from a family where there was more fi fighting, rebellion or compliance than negotiating.

- You feel discouraged, awkward, or worried.
- You may agree and then not follow through.

All of these problems are solvable, and this chapter is designed to show you how to overcome these barriers and agree to negotiate with your partner.

Skills for Cooperation

Working together to solve conflicts may be a totally new concept to both of you. Not only does it require a new way of thinking about problem solving, but it also requires a new set of skills which may be new to you including how to:

4. Become comfortable with cooperation techniques and get familiar with them, so your old habits don't take over.
5. Communicate clearly, with I messages active listening and attentive speaking instead of criticism and defensiveness.
6. Reassure each other to minimize struggling.
7. Persist gently instead of giving up or getting angry; and, (if your partner cannot or will not work with you,)
8. Find your own solution without your partner's help, so you don't have to feel helpless, dissatisfied and angry.

The exercises and guidelines will teach you the skills you need to communicate clearly, understand your partner better, persist gently, and overcome competing and struggling. If you feel stuck at any point, there is a Trouble Shooting Guide at the end of this chapter which will help you determine what's in the way and how to resolve it.

Effective Communication

Effective communication can help you overcome inexperience and mistrust, because you can explain why working together will be beneficial to both of you. At the same time, it will help you become more effective at Reassuring, Overcoming Rescues and Persisting, because all of those skills require communication.

You have already seen in chapter three that how you communicate your problem is crucial to being heard. In this chapter you will learn communication techniques that will help you:

- keep your communication cooperative, rather than competitive,
- reassure each other when fear blocks your problem solving,
- keep your conversation focused on getting information and solving the problem rather than arguing.

The Basics of Communication

When you express your thoughts and feelings as facts about yourself ("I feel scared", rather than "you scared me") it leads to agreement, because your partner will be more open to empathize and care about what you feel; but phrasing it as criticism of your partner (you don't love me) leads to conflict, because your partner will feel attacked and defensive. Here are some examples of statements or questions that Michelle and Lou could use in their effort to negotiate about housework. Read the following parallel conversations and feel your reaction to the statements on each side. See if you can understand why we've categorized them under Conflict Creating or Agreement Creating.

Conflict Creating or	Agreement Creating
Michelle: You condescend to me and I don't like it.	When you make a joke about something I do, I feel bad.
Lou: I'm just joking. Can't you take it?	Do you feel put down when I joke about you?
Michelle: Why are you such a bully? You put me down and when I complain, you put me down again.	You're right; I do feel bad if you joke about me.
Lou: Look, when I joke around, I don't really mean it. You should know that by now.	I don't mean to make you feel bad, it's just that when you do something absent-minded, I feel like teasing you.

Conflict Creating

Michelle: I think you do mean it. I think you want to punish me for fouling up.

Lou: What a bunch of bull!

Michelle: Forget it. I'm not going to talk to you.

Agreement Creating

You feel like teasing me, but to me it feels like criticism. Maybe I already feel bad, so your joke really hurts.

Wow, I had no idea it hurt you so much. I'll be more careful about joking. Now, do you want to get back to talking about the problem?

Thank you. I'll try not to be so sensitive. And yes, let's get back to the housekeeping issue.

While it may seem difficult to make such rational Agreement Creating statements in the midst of a conflict, it is not as hard as it looks, and certainly not as damaging to your relationship or difficult as dealing with constant conflict. If you review the Conflict Creating statements, you will find they exhibit several attitudes:

- *Defensive:* When either of you feels attacked, you'll be busy denying that you're to blame, and not listening to each other.
- *Argumentative:* When you focus more on who's right or wrong or whether the problem is real instead of focusing on how to work together to solve the problem.
- *Objecting:* When you counter each of your partner's statements with a counter-argument instead of listening and trying to understand, or criticize your partner's opinion instead of listening, or
- *Critical judgment:* When your responses are about what's wrong with your partner instead of what your partner is saying.

All the above attitudes will be more likely to get a hostile, resistant response because they are negative and attacking, which prompts the listener to counter-attack. Therefore, the longer this conversation goes on, the more argumentative, negative and uncooperative it gets.

Both Michelle and Lou have a better chance of reaching an agreement to negotiate with the agreement creating statements in the right hand column, which have four elements in common:

1. They demonstrate that you're listening because they reflect back what your partner said, which is reassuring to your partner, diffuses defensiveness and invites a similar, thoughtful response.

2. They give or request non-judgmental, factual I message information.

3. They are short and simple, so they can be easily understood.

4. They are calm and thoughtful, rather than dramatic, emotional or reactive.

Knowing how phrase what you say in negotiation can help you reduce the length and frequency of your arguments and power struggles, because you'll be calming, reassuring and informative. When your interaction minimizes conflict and promotes sharing and listening: each of you will learn new things about yourself and your partner, and your discussion is more enjoyable. Each successful negotiation makes the next agreement to negotiate easier because you'll have a positive feeling about the process and each other.

The agreement creating skills are:

- I messages: How to give information that is easy to hear and understand about what you feel and what you want.

- Active listening: How to listen and play back what your partner said for confirmation that it's what was meant.

- Attentive speaking: How to make sure that the information received was what you intended to send.

Learning these three skills can change your whole experience of talking from frustrating, volatile, argumentative and futile (conflict based) exercises into calm, satisfying, effective and cooperative (agreement based) discussions that accomplish what you intend to do.

I Messages

Notice how the sentences that begin with I in the agreement creating column are easy to hear. It is much less threatening to your partner when you say "I feel hurt" or even "I feel angry" than if you say "You hurt me", or "You make me mad". When you own your feelings by saying "I", your partner is less likely to feel blamed and get defensive and more likely to empathize and understand. By saying how you feel rather than blaming and accusing, you are much more likely to be understood.

I messages avoid the critical, attacking, defensiveness-creating atmosphere that You messages create. You messages consist of perceptions or judgments about the other person, usually couched in a critical, or even abusive, manner ("You didn't do that right"," You look terrible", "you made me so mad I wanted to hit you"). Of course, positive you messages, (such as "You're beautiful", "you look great in that hat", "you did a great job", and "you have a lovely smile") usually do not create problems, so it's only the negative, critical you messages we're talking about. Negative you are upsetting; they create defensiveness, and prevent your partner from listening or understanding.

Negative you messages are very difficult to hear because when we feel criticized and accused we naturally get defensive, focus on counter-attacking, and stop listening to the other person. I statements, however, are easier to hear: "I feel defensive" is easier to hear than "you are attacking me." "I don't want to clean up the kitchen" is easier to hear than "You left a mess in the kitchen."

I messages are effective because they communicate information about you in a way that minimizes argument. By using I messages, you express what you think, feel, see and hear without projecting your feelings onto your partner: "I'd like to go out with you more often" instead of "You never want to go out with me anymore." I messages can be positive, too. ("I love you", "I feel great about the way we work together", "I am very satisfied with this decision"). Sharing information about yourself, your feelings, your ideas and your reactions in this way helps your partner to understand you, your ideas and feelings. I messages can also be clear and direct: it works better to say "I would like some time alone": instead of sighing and saying (passively) "Gee it's so hard to get enough time alone." or (indirectly) "Don't you have to leave now?"

The following exercise will help you develop your I messages skills, clarify what you want to say, and make it easier for you to be heard by your partner when you have a problem or a disagreement.

Exercise: Turning You Messages into I Messages

1. Make a List:

Review your relationship history and either a) develop a list of you messages that created problems in the past, or b) observe yourself and your partner for a few days, and record on paper any you messages you hear.

2. Practice:

Divide a piece of paper into two columns, as in the following example. Write the You messages you collected in the left column and then practice turning each you message into an I message, as shown.

Here are some examples to get you started:

You Message	Becomes I Message
You never take out the trash.	I want you to take out the trash as often as I do
You aren't home enough.	I feel lonely and wonder if you still love me
You don't spend enough time with me anymore.	I miss sharing time with you and I'm worried you don't care anymore.
You don't pay your share of the bills.	I want to renegotiate our financial agreement.
Are you cheating on me?	I feel insecure and suspicious

because we aren't having sex.

Active Listening

I messages will help you speak more effectively, and Active Listening can help you hear your partner better. When you ask for an agreement to negotiate, and your partner refuses, objects or avoids answering, Active Listening can help you understand any resistance, so you can effectively reassure your partner and create the agreement you want. It also means listening the way you'd like to be listened to. To do this, you take turns repeating in your own words what your partner says to demonstrate you are listening carefully, and to verify that you understood as in the following guidelines.

Guidelines for Active Listening

1. Read the Signs:

Learn to recognize when your partner has something significant to discuss. If you notice a change in your partner's emotional attitude or demeanor, (for example, your normally talkative or cheerful partner becomes quiet, sullen or depressed, or snaps at you for no real reason, or is reluctant to discuss and issue or negotiate with you), he or she is probably troubled about something. Let your partner know that you care about his or her feelings and objections by gently asking for information about it: "Is there something you want to talk about?" or "Do you have a problem with what I said?" or "Is there a reason why you don't want to do this?" Ask, show your interest and caring, allow time for an answer, but don't push or insist.

2. Listen and Repeat:

Do your best to pay attention to what your partner is saying. You know you have succeeded in understanding what your partner means when you can repeat what you heard and your partner confirms it. For example, if your partner says "You won't listen to what I want anyway," instead of arguing with that, just say "You believe I won't care about what you want?" If your partner says that's what he or she meant, you have just reassured him or her that you're listening.

If not, keep rephrasing what you heard (or asking your partner to repeat it) until your partner confirms that is what he or she meant.

3. Ask Questions:

Ask questions if you don't understand. If your partner is going on at length, you might say, "Could you stop a minute? I want to be sure I understand your last point before you go on to the next." Then *repeat* what you have heard so far, and get confirmation that you heard it the way your partner meant it. Don't allow yourself to become overwhelmed by a torrent of words or confusing statements; ask for explanations when you need them.

4. Listening is Not Agreeing:

Remember that listening to your partner does not necessarily mean you agree. Even if you still disagree, you'll have a better chance of solving the problem because you have a clear understanding of the opposing ideas. Saying "tell me more" is a wonderful way to be attentive to your partner when you are not sure you agree, but want to understand what is going on before you question or challenge your partner's statements. You may find that you simply misunderstood what your partner said at first, or that you're not as opposed to your partner's ideas as you thought.

5. Take Responsibility:

If it seems to you that active listening means you have to take responsibility for both sides of the conversation, you're right, to a degree. Communication works best when both speaker and listener take responsibility for being heard as well as for hearing. While this may sound like a lot of work in the beginning, it will soon become obvious how much easier it is than arguing, fighting and not communicating.

Here are some examples of I messages and active listening in action:

Michelle: When you make a joke about a mistake I made, I feel hurt and criticized. (I message)

Lou: (paraphrasing; active listening) Do you feel put down when I joke about you?

Michelle: Yes, I do. (confirmation)

Carol: (I message) I feel like I do all the housework and all the caring around here alone.

Joe: (paraphrasing; active listening) Sounds like you feel overworked and not cared about. (asking for information) Tell me more about that, I want to understand.

Don: (I message) I'm going to start riding my bike to work on Thursdays so I can save time getting to night class.

Dale: (critical, negative response) It's too dangerous. That's a terrible neighborhood and the traffic is fast and furious.

Don: (active listening) You're afraid I'll get hurt?

Dale: (calmer, confirms) Yes. It's too dangerous. I don't want you to get hurt.

Don: (asking for Agreement to Negotiate) I don't want you to be worried. Do you want to discuss the problem?

Dale: (relieved) Yes. I'd like to have some say in your decision, too.

Michelle: (I message) Lou, I'm getting more and more uncomfortable about how we act with each other. I feel frustrated, unappreciated and criticized.

Lou: (defensive) Well, why don't you talk back? Why don't you stand up for yourself? I'm not doing anything wrong.

Michelle: (active listening; paraphrase) Do you think I'm accusing you of doing something wrong?

Lou: (confirming) It sure sounds like it.

Michelle: (I message) I don't want to accuse you, I care about you and our relationship, I see a problem that could get out of hand, and

I'd like your help fixing it. (asking for agreement) Will you help me figure out what's wrong and what we both can do about it?

Lou: (calmer, but still wary) Well, when you put it that way, I guess I'll try.

Sometimes, active listening makes it clear that someone doesn't quite understand; which gives you opportunity to clarify it, as in the following interchange between Michelle and Lou:

Michelle: (hurt, using I messages) When you made a joke about how I broke the blender last night, I felt embarrassed and incompetent. It's happened a lot and it's a serious problem for me.

Lou: (confused, paraphrasing) You're feeling bad because I comment on mistakes you make?

Michelle: (explains more clearly) Yes, but it's more the way you comment. When you make a joke, I feel like you're putting me down. It's an awful feeling.

Lou: (catching on, paraphrasing again) Being made fun of is the problem?

Michelle: (confirming) Yes.

Lou: (offering to negotiate) Now I understand. I didn't realize that my teasing upset you, and I wondered why you were so cold to me afterward. Do you want to see if we can sort it out?

Michelle: (agreeing to negotiate) Yes, I'd like to get it cleared up. It's creating problems for us.

Active listening allowed Michelle and Lou to get by a potential argument and clarify what was being said enough to reach an agreement to negotiate.

Attentive Speaking

The third component of effective communication is attentive speaking. A lot has been written about active listening; but attentive speaking is less well known and less understood. It is a simple and highly effective technique will help you communicate better with your partner, too.

Attentive speaking simply means paying attention to how your partner is receiving what you say. If you watch carefully, your partner's facial expression, body movements, and posture will provide clues (looking interested, fidgeting, looking bored, eyes wandering, attempting to interrupt, facial expressions of anger or confusion, or a blank, empty stare) to help you know whether you are being understood.

The guidelines here will help you observe whether you are successfully communicating what you want your partner to hear, without any verbal communication from your partner.

This is especially effective if your partner:

- is not very talkative,
- thinks disagreeing, or objecting will hurt your feelings
- is the unemotional, strong, silent type,
- is easily overwhelmed in a discussion,

or

- is passive, depressed, or withdrawn.

Sometimes, your partner will be reluctant to share a negative reaction to what you are saying. If your partner becomes more and more upset by what you are saying, stops listening, gets confused, mentally objects, silently argues with you, or withdraws, you need to know. If you don't use attentive speaking to see the clues, your partner may surprise you and react with anger, misunderstand you or just not be interested in listening anymore, and all your efforts to communicate are wasted. These guidelines will help you figure out when you aren't communicating well or getting the reaction you want.

Using Attentive Speaking will help you:

- avoid overwhelming your partner with too much information at once, (you will notice when he or she looks overwhelmed, bored or distracted)
- keep your partner's interest in what you have to say, (you can ask a question when you see your partner's attention slipping away)

- understand when what you say is misunderstood, (you can watch facial expressions and notice when they're different than what you expect)
- gauge your partner's reaction when he or she doesn't say anything (watch facial expressions, body language and attentiveness)
- tell when your partner is too distracted, stressed or upset to really hear what you're saying (watch facial expressions, body language and attentiveness)

Guidelines for Attentive Speaking

1. Watch your listener.

When it is important to you to communicate effectively, keep your eyes on your partner's face and body, which will let your partner know you care if her or she hears you, increase your partner's tendency to make eye contact with you, and therefore cause him or her to listen more carefully.

2. Understand the clues:

Clues in your partner's facial expression (a smile, a frown, a glassy-eyed stare) body position (upright and alert, slumped and sullen, turned away from you and inattentive) and movements (leaning toward you, pulling away from you, fidgeting, restlessness) tell you how you are being received. For example, if you say "I love you" and you observe that your partner turns away and looks out the window, the clues indicate that you weren't received the way you wanted to be. Either your partner is too distracted to hear you, or he or she is having a problem with what you said.

3. Ask questions:

If you get a response that seems unusual or inappropriate to what you said, (you think you're giving a complement, and your partner looks confused, hurt or angry; or you think you're stating objective facts and your partner looks like he or she disagrees; you're angry, but your partner is smiling) ask a gentle question. For example: "I thought I was giving you a complement, but you look annoyed. Did I say something wrong?" Or, "Gee, I thought you'd be happy to hear this but you look upset. Please tell me what you're thinking." Or, "What you just said sounded angry, but you're smiling. Did I misunderstand you?" Or, just "Do you agree?"

4. Watch for overload:

If your partner becomes fidgety or looks off into space as you talk, either what you're saying is emotionally uncomfortable for your partner, the time is not good for talking (business pressures, stress, the ball game is on), your partner is bored or you've been talking too long. If it looks like your partner is bored, invite your partner to comment: "What do you think?" or "Do you see it the same way?" or perhaps "Am I talking too much (or too fast)?" If you think it's a bad time, just ask: "You look distracted. Is this a good time to talk about this?" (If it is a bad time, then make a date to talk at a better time, or just begin again later)

5. Notice Confusion:

When you're paying attention as you speak, incomprehension and confusion are easy to spot. If your partner has a blank or glassy-eyed look, or looks worried or confused, you may be putting out too many ideas all at once, or you may not be explaining your thoughts clearly enough. Again, ask a question: "Am I making sense to you?" "Am I going too fast?" or, "Do you have any questions?" Sometimes, just a pause in what you are saying will give your partner the room to ask a question and clear up confusion.

6. Don't Blame:

Blaming your listener by insisting that he or she just isn't paying enough attention will only exacerbate the problem. Instead, ask a question, such as "I don't think I'm explaining this clearly; have I lost you?" or "Am I bringing up too many things at once?" Phrasing the questions to show that you're looking for ways to improve your style and clarity invites cooperation and encourages teamwork.

With active speaking you can find out immediately if you are communicating well with your partner. If you see signs of confusion or trouble, as Lou does in the following example, you can put things back on track quite easily.

After a busy period when Michelle and Lou haven't had much time for relaxation or with each other, they are in the kitchen getting breakfast before work.

Lou: Hey, Michelle, I sure love you.

Michelle: (Looks out the window and says nothing)

Lou: (attentive speaking, asks for response) Hello? Michelle, did you hear me? You looked away. Are you just tired, or is there a problem?

Michelle: (angry) I was thinking "talk is cheap" but I didn't want to say it.

Lou: (active listening, paraphrase) Do you mean, you don't believe that I love you?

Michelle: (calmer, using mostly I messages) Oh, I know you love me. It's just that I've felt neglected lately. You haven't been attentive, we haven't spent any time together, and I've missed it. Saying "I love you" isn't enough.

Lou: (acknowledging, asking for negotiation) You're right. We've been way too busy, and I miss you, too. Let's take some time off Saturday from chores and things, and sit down and discuss our schedule, so we can make more time for us.

Michelle: (Agrees to Negotiate) We do need to figure some things out, and it would be nice to talk. It's a date for Saturday.

Lou's attentive speaking made him aware that Michelle didn't respond, and because of it, they were able to make an agreement to negotiate.

I messages, active listening and attentive speaking can improve your communication so much that you can usually overcome most of the barriers to getting an agreement to negotiate, because your partner will feel cared about and listened to, and will not be as likely to get defensive, competitive or argumentative. As you practice following the guidelines and become familiar with these effective communication skills, you'll find them very useful in all the steps of cooperative negotiation, in many of the exercises in the book, and even in your conversations with friends, family and business associates.

Barriers to Agreeing to Negotiate

Even when you have good communication skills, you can fail to reach agreement because you encounter barriers, which are attitudes, beliefs and old habit patterns that can make it difficult or impossible to move through the various steps to getting an Agreement to Negotiate. At these times, one or both of you can seem:

- stubborn and unreasonable,
- hopeless and depressed,
- unable to communicate even though you've learned the necessary skills,
- so afraid or anxious that you cannot be reassured, or
- unable to stop arguing and begin problem-solving.

When these signs occur, you needn't panic or be discouraged. It simply means that you have encountered some of the barriers to agreeing to negotiate. You can learn to overcome each barrier and once you develop the skills presented in this chapter, you will find getting to an agreement to negotiate with your partner much easier, even when the problem you are presenting is difficult or complicated.

The most common barriers people encounter in trying to work together are: Inexperience and Mistrust, the Power Struggle Habit, and The Rescue.

Trust, Inexperience and Mistrust

It is much easier to learn to solve problems together easily when you allow yourselves to be beginners and learn the skills, and have extra patience with the process and each other as you try these new ideas.

In the first dialogue in this chapter, Michelle was able to state her problem, but forgot to ask for a negotiation. In the second example, she asked, but failed to notice that Lou had not agreed. However, after taking time to learn the skills of gentle persistence, clear communication and reassurance, Michelle could use these skills to enlist Lou in a negotiation:

Michelle: (clear communication) Lou, I'm getting more and more unhappy about how you talk down to me sometimes. I think we're both contributing to the problem and I want us to sit down and see if we can sort it out and find a way of being together that feels better.

Lou: (shrugging her off) That doesn't seem necessary, I'll just try to be nicer from now on.

Michelle: (gentle persistence) That's not what I had in mind. We tried that Cooperative problem solving method before and I want to use it for this problem. It involves both of us, so we need to agree to negotiate about it before we can go ahead.

Lou: (resisting) Seems like a lot to go through just because I criticize you sometimes. Why don't I just try to shape up a little and let's see how it goes?

Michelle: (more persistence and clear communication) Lou, this is important and I think we're both going to have to make a change or two, and it doesn't involve being nicer. I want to agree on the changes we are both going to make, and I think you will want the same thing in order to resolve this. Will you reserve some time for negotiating this? I believe it will be worth it.

Lou: (doubtful) Sounds ominous. I don't know.

Michelle: (reassuring) I'm starting to feel like a nag, but I want you to understand that this is for us both. Remember, that the purpose of negotiating is so that we both get what we want. We're not finished until we both feel good about the outcome. How about giving it a try?

Lou: (reassured, agreeing) You're very convincing. If you keep this up, I'll have to quit teasing you about not knowing anything. Ok, let's give it a shot. When do we start?

When Lou has successfully negotiated a number of issues with

Michelle and sees that he gets what he wants, he will know from first-hand experience that the process works, and how to do it. With practice, you and your partner will also learn where you are likely to get into difficulties and how to remedy them. As you find yourself succeeding more often, your confidence in cooperative problem solving will grow, making it easy to agree to negotiate.

Overcoming Inexperience and Mistrust

Joe and Carol are new at working together on problems, and Joe sees no benefit to himself in negotiating the problem with Carol, so he's reluctant to begin. If you like the way things are, like Joe in the following dialogue, and (like Carol) your partner wants a change, it might be difficult to agree to negotiate.

Carol: (stating problem, asking for negotiation) Joe, I'm feeling burdened and overworked because I work and do all the housework, too. Will you help me figure out a way to cut my work load?

Joe: (resisting negotiation) Anything you come up with is OK with me as long as I don't have to do any housework. I'm much too tired for that.

Carol: (asks more clearly) What I want is your help in solving the problem. It's a problem that affects us both and I want you to participate in coming up with a solution.

Joe: (refuses shifts focus) Well, I like the way things are, so it looks like only you have a problem.

The Power Struggle Habit

Many couples believe solving relationship problems means a struggle in which one partner may win the specific issue, but both of you end up unsatisfied and sometimes resentful, so it's not surprising if either or both of you would be unwilling to even try to negotiate for fear of reaching the same old outcome, which looks like one of these:

Guilt and Obligation:

This is the familiar "if you loved me, you'd..." or "how can you do that to me (expect that of me, not do that for me)" gambit. One partner uses guilt or obligation to coerce the other into doing something.

Threats and Emotional Blackmail:

This is the opposite of guilt. Rather than saying "If you loved me..." the attitude here is "If you don't do what I want, I won't love you." In extreme cases, this can become very overbearing and abusive.

Courtroom Logic:

This is a relentless argument, lawyer-style, where one partner attempts to prove a case or be right, and deserve to get what they want. The argument sounds very logical, but it is completely one-sided and does not take the other partner's wants, feelings and needs into account. In fact, it often belittles or quasi-logically dismisses them.

Keeping the Peace:

Passive partners try to be nice and give in to the above manipulations to keep the peace by never saying what they want for fear it will upset their partner.

Compromising:

Both partners give up some of what they want in order to reach agreement. It is time-honored as the best way to solve problems, but couples who do it usually find that resentment builds as they give up what they want bit by bit.

Hammering Away:

This is relentless persistence without gentleness or consideration for the other's wants, often called nagging, badgering and harassment. One partner just keeps insisting on getting what he or she wants, until the other gives in.

A competitive power struggle approach to problem-solving is never pleasant for either partner. Even if the winner sometimes feels good about getting what he or she wants, there are unpleasant repercussions later when anger and resentment build up in the losing partner until it erupts in rage, depression or separation. So, if problem-solving has meant struggles like this in your history, it is quite easy to see why you or your partner might be hesitant to agree to begin the process.

When you ask for a negotiation, your partner might be suspicious that the offer is an attempt to manipulate, especially if the two of you have a history of power struggles together. Dale, who is well aware that he and Don have a history of power struggles, reacts suspiciously to Don's offer to negotiate:

Don: I've been thinking about your idea of using the back bedroom for your office, and I'd like to use it for my office, too.

Dale: But it isn't big enough for both of us. What's the matter with your office on Main Street?

Don: I'd like to negotiate about this to see if we can both get what we want.

Dale: Negotiate? I don't know what I would do for an office if you had the back bedroom. Why do you need to give up your office on Main?

Don: If we negotiate, like in the book, maybe we can both be happy.

Dale: Not if you get that room and I have to stay in the dining room.

Don: Look, if I get the back bedroom, and that makes you unhappy, then we haven't done Cooperative Negotiation. Both of us have to be happy for the negotiation to be successful. Let's try it and see how it works.

Dale: I can tell you right now, I won't be happy if you get that room and I don't. No way.

In the above example, Dale is clearly refusing to negotiate. At other times, the refusal may not be so clear. Here is how Dale might refuse in an indirect or covert way.

Don: It looks like we both have our eyes on the back bedroom for an office. What do you say we try to find an answer?

Dale: I'm busy, not right now, sorry.

-- Later --

Don: Want to talk about the back bedroom office situation?

Dale: I've got a lot of work to do.

Dale is not clearly saying he doesn't want to negotiate because he's not sure himself. He's feeling nervous about it, so he's just avoiding the subject in any way he can.

The following guidelines and exercises for overcoming the power struggle habit will help you overcome your natural resistance to struggling and replace it with confidence in mutual cooperation.

Reassurance and Overcoming the Power Struggle Habit

When you and your partner are accustomed to power struggles, your agreement to negotiate can be blocked by the fear that the negotiation will be just another tussle, which you'll lose and be the bad guy. Worse yet, after all the hassle, frustration and resentment, the problem could still be unsolved. Determining the source of the fear (is it fear of losing? fear of arguing or fighting? fear it won't work?) gives you an idea about what is needed to reassure each other, as in the following step-by-step guideline.

Reluctance or refusal to agree to problem solving is usually the result of one or more specific fears, such as:

- Fear of being manipulated or overpowered.
- Fear of being taken advantage of, made a fool of, or conned
- Fear of having another fight
- Fear that the process will be a long, complicated hassle (hard work) without a worthwhile result (a waste of time)
- Fear of losing, or having to give up something important.
- Fear that cooperative negotiation (because it's a new approach) won't go well or work at all.

Each of these fears, and any others that might come up, can be discovered, communicated and reassured with these guidelines.

Guidelines for Reassurance

Step 1. Find out what your partner's fears are:

If your partner won't agree to negotiate with you, don't just guess what's wrong; because you will confuse both of you, and increase your partner's resistance. Instead:

A. *Tell your partner what you observe:* ("we agreed to take turns taking out the garbage, and you haven't done your share", "when I ask you to negotiate, you say you're busy").

B. *Check your thinking:* Because you are using you messages in part A, be sure you let your partner know that you're just explaining what you observe, and ask your partner if what you see is correct, and what it means.

C. *Ask again to negotiate:* If your partner denies that he or she is reluctant, ask again if the two of you can negotiate, since there is no reason why not.

D. *Use active listening:* If your partner acknowledges (admits) being scared, ask what the reluctance to negotiate is about. Whatever your partner says, don't argue about it. Listen to the answers carefully, and use active listening to find out the reason for the refusal.

E. *Acknowledge your own fears:* Read the list of fears you created together to see what fits. Acknowledge your own fears (as well as your partner's) as you read the list. To get fears into the open where they can be reassured, it is often helpful to consider what the worst possible outcome of agreeing to negotiate could be, and allow your imagination to run wild (What if you find out you're incompatible and you have to break up? What if you get into such a bad fight you don't talk for days?). If either of you are having such scary thoughts, it's better you get them into the open, where you can figure out how to handle those unlikely events if they do happen.

On the left-hand side of a piece of paper, make a list of the fears or fantasies that stop you and your partner from using Cooperative

Negotiation. When your list is complete, you are ready to move on to reassurance, in Step 2.

Here's how Don uses these guidelines (informally) in response to Dale.

Don: (offer to negotiate) Will you work this home office problem out with me?

Dale: (avoids issue) Maybe later. I'm reading right now.

Don: (lets Dale know what Don thinks is happening) Dale, I've invited you several times to work this out, and I think you're avoiding it. Will you tell me why you keep putting me off?

Dale: (begins to express fear) I don't want to get into it. Why should I? If we talk about it, you'll just win the argument. I won't get anything I want.

Don: (acknowledges fear by paraphrasing it, with active listening.) You think I'm going to try to talk you out of using the back bedroom?

Dale: (relaxes a little, less defensive) Yes. You've tried it before.

Don: (more acknowledgment) You're right, I guess I have overpowered you in discussions before. And now you're afraid I'm going to try it again?

Dale: Yes.

Don is clear now that the problem is Dale's fear (from past experience) that Don will overpower him. Now, can proceed to the next step and reassure Dale about what he has learned about the importance of both of them getting what they want.

Step 2: Reassure Your Partner

If you can reassure your partner that the negotiation itself will not be unpleasant, and it won't lead to something bad, there will be nothing to fear, and your negotiation can be a pleasant experience with a desirable outcome, the resistance could turn to enthusiasm. If you and your partner can't agree to negotiate because of your history of power struggling, reassurance will smooth the way. The following exercise will show you how to reassure your partner.

1. Reassure each fear:

In Step One, you determined your partner's fears. Now, you can begin to reassure each one.

Consider each fear on the list and ask your partner what would reassure him or her and reduce the resistance. Figure out together how you would handle the situation if the worst fears came true ("If the argument got so bad we weren't talking, we could see a counselor"). When you have a strategy to take care of yourselves, you'll have the confidence to try negotiation. If any of the fears are based on things that have happened before, acknowledge that they did happen, and explain what is different now ("You're right, I did get angry and yell before, but I've realized that doesn't get me what I want, and I've learned to control my anger better"). On the list of fears from Step 1, write the solutions or reassurances for each fear, as in the examples below:

Fear	Reassurance
You're trying to manipulate me.	I have in the past, but not this time.
You're conning me	I want to try this negotiation method and see if we both can really get what we want.
You'll try to overpower me	The solution doesn't count if either of us doesn't like it.
We'll just end up fighting and this will be another hassle	If we start arguing instead of negotiating, we'll just take a break.
I'll have to give up something	If you don't like our solution it won't count; and you can even change your mind later
This is going to be hard work and a waste of time	It may be hard work because we have to learn how to do it, but if it works, it'll make our
I just don't trust this negotiation thing.	

life a lot easier.
Since our solution doesn't

count if we aren't both happy, what can we lose by trying it?

When you have reassured each fear on the list, you are ready to go on to Step 3.

Once you get more accustomed to reassuring your partner, it can be done much more informally, as Don reassures Dale in the rest of their discussion.

Don: (more acknowledgment) You're right, I guess I have overpowered you in discussions before. And now you're afraid I'm going to try it again?

Dale: Yes.

Don: (acknowledging and reassuring Dale's fear) I can understand how you'd think I was trying to argue you out of using that room, because I've done that before over different issues. I know I've used anger, silence and shouting to win arguments before. But now I've learned some new things, and I realize that my old ways of winning have damaged the relationship. I want to try this cooperative negotiation where we would work together to come up with a solution we both like.

Dale: (still afraid) Yeah, but what if I don't like the solution?

Don: (reassures again) Then we keep working on it until we have a solution we both like.

Dale: (not sure) Sounds too good to be true.

Don: (acknowledging, reassuring) I know. But I think it's worth a try. We won't agree on anything that doesn't suit us both and if we can't do it, we'll be no worse off than we are now.

Dale: (one last fear) Are you setting me up?

Don: (one more reassurance) No. I really want you to be happy with our solution. Will you give me a chance to show you, by trying a negotiation with me?

Dale: (agrees, with reservations) OK, but if you yell or get mad, I'm quitting.

Don: Ok, it's a deal.

Dale has been clear about his concerns and Don was able to respond directly, using the guidelines in an informal way. While Dale's agreement is not enthusiastic, it opens a chance to try Cooperative Negotiation, and let the experience itself prove that it works.

Step 3. Ask for Agreement to Negotiate.

Once you and your partner are reassured that you will not fall into your old Power Struggle Habit, the resistance to negotiating should subside. Now you can begin again by asking for an Agreement to Negotiate, and moving on into Cooperative Negotiation, like Don and Dale do here:

Don: I really want you to be happy with our solution. How can I reassure you?

Dale: Show me, I guess.

Don: Well, if we try negotiating, and I don't overpower you, will that show you?

Dale: Yeah, I guess so.

Don: Ok, let's negotiate this bedroom office problem.

Dale: I don't have to agree with your idea if I don't like it, and you won't get angry?

Don: No, because I want you to be happy, too. As long as you are willing to try to solve the problem with me, I won't try to push you into doing what I want.

Dale: In that case, I'm willing to try negotiating.

At this point, Don and Dale have overcome the major part of Dale's fears about power struggles, and they can begin by working together on problem solving.

As you practice reassuring yourself and your partner, you'll find it gets easier to do, and the more reassurance you give each other, the easier and smoother your negotiation will be. Reassurance will come up again and again throughout the book, because it can be useful when you are having trouble with any of the steps of negotiation.

The Rescue

If one of you is accustomed to giving in, sacrificing, or compromising as a way to resolve conflicts, you may derail the negotiation process before it ever gets started by not letting your partner know what you want, or by giving in without negotiating, which we call a rescue.

You are rescuing when you:

- give away all or part of what you want,
- attempt to guess or anticipate your partner's wants, without considering your own,
- try to please your partner regardless of what you want,
- let your partner's real or imagined wants be more important to you than your own.
- give in before problem solving begins, as a way of avoiding painful power struggles.

People who don't want confrontation will avoid agreeing to negotiate if they can, so they rescue instead of trying direct negotiating. If you compromise, give in, or do a favor with a sense of sacrifice, resentment or superiority over your partner, then your action is a rescue.

To reach a mutually satisfactory negotiation, both people need to know and ask for exactly what they want. Letting the other person have their way may sound like being nice, cooperating, or caring, but it leads to dissatisfaction and destructive resentment.

Rescuing and being rescued are so common you may think it's the way you should be in your relationship Often the relationships we observe (as well as those in lots of books, plays, movies, and songs) are built on rescuing and being rescued. Even though many people do it, and many think you should do it, rescuing and being rescued is dysfunctional: it doesn't work.

You can't negotiate when one of you insists "There's no problem, we'll do it your way." or "Never mind what I suggested, I'd rather do what you want" because you both need to know what each of you wants.

When you propose to negotiate and your partner just gives in, that's saying no to negotiating; often equivalent of saying I would rather be dissatisfied than negotiate. You can do this occasionally without creating a serious problem, but if it happens too often, the rescuer will become dissatisfied and resentful, eventually thinking "after all I've done for you..." or, "if you loved me, you'd ....”

When Carol tries to get an Agreement to Negotiate from Joe, he puts up a rescue barrier:

Carol: (frustrated) I feel like I do all the housework and all the caring around here and there's no one to help me or even take up some of the housework slack. Will you help me sort this out and find a solution that works for both of us?

Joe: (feeling overburdened at work, but not saying so; avoiding the discussion at all costs) Ok, Ok, I'll do the housework this week.

If Carol accepts this as a solution to the problem, Joe will probably be in a bad mood all week, do the housework begrudgingly or poorly, and/or forget his promise, because he's rescuing to avoid problem solving, and he has no real desire to help.

You can also rescue silently; not bring a problem up for negotiation at all. For example, Fred might say to himself: "I'd join the Thursday night computer class, but it costs money and Naomi likes us to spend our evenings together, so I'll just forget it." Without Naomi's knowledge, Fred has rescued her. If he does this often, he'll eventually feel that Naomi keeps him restricted and he never gets to do what he wants, and Naomi will wonder why he seems resentful.

Fred never asked Naomi what her feeling was about his taking a class. She might have welcomed the chance to have an evening to herself, to see friends, or to take some classes on her own. She may have been excited for him, and eager to support and encourage him. But, if she doesn't say so, and Fred never tells her he'd like to take a class, both of them can feel restless, restricted and deprived. Neither of them will be fully aware that decisions have been made without discussion, and both will feel confused and dissatisfied with their Thursday evenings together.

You can even rescue your partner by having a one-sided conversation out loud, as Carol does here:

Carol: I'm beat tonight and I don't feel like doing the dishes. Can we work a deal?

Joe: (silence. He's focused on his tablet)

Carol: You're probably tired, too.

Joe: (still silent, oblivious)

Carol: What if I just stack the dishes and if you don't feel like doing them, I'll wash them in the morning.

Joe: OK.

Carol has neatly argued herself into not asking for Joe's help in solving the problem about the dishes, and once again, left herself solely responsible for the housework, which she resents, and Joe is content: He is getting what he wants for the moment, and is not aware of Carol's resentment. However, he may pay a price later as a frustrated and angry Carol becomes grumpy, withholds sex, or gets angry over small things.

Of course, not every time you and your partner agree is a rescue. Sometimes you truly agree with what your partner wants, so you are already getting what you want and a negotiation is unnecessary. If you feel satisfied, generous and loving, and want your partner to get what he or she wants and are not going to feel bad, deprived, or ripped off about it later, you are giving and not rescuing. You can tell when it is genuine generosity, rather than a rescue, because the giver feels good about it, not deprived or resentful.

Overcoming the Rescue

If either of you is dissatisfied or resentful and you don't seem to be able to discuss things with each other, then rescuing is probably your problem. The following checklist will help you discover if you are a rescuer or if you are being rescued, and teach you how to change these destructive patterns so that you can have a much greater degree of mutual satisfaction in your relationship.

Checklist: Rescue Discovery

The following checklist will help you decide if you are a rescuer, or you are allowing yourself to be rescued. Just check the statements that apply to you.

You are rescuing if you:

- Believe you must do something for your partner that he or she can do alone, without being asked or giving them a chance to refuse. "I hate cooking, but Dale would starve to death if I didn't cook a good meal every night."

- Do something that you do not want to do for or because of your partner, and feel resentful later. (See Carol and Joe's one-sided dialogue just above)

- Do not ask for what you want, because you fear your partner's reaction to the request, you can't take no for an answer, or you believe your partner is incapable of saying no. (Fred doesn't ask Naomi about taking a class on Thursdays)

- Act as if your partner is incapable, put him or her in the child role, and act as a parent (giving unsolicited advice, giving orders, nagging, or criticizing)

- Do not tell your partner when something he or she does or says is a problem for you; not asking for what you want your partner to do differently. (Rose resents John's bringing business associates home on short notice; but doesn't say anything.)

- Contribute more than 50% of the effort to any project or activity that is supposed to be mutual, (including housework, earning income, making dates and social plans, initiating sex, carrying the conversations, giving comfort and support) without an agreement that your extra efforts will be specifically and adequately rewarded or compensated.

- Feel your role is to fix, protect, control, feel for, worry about, ignore the expressed wants of, or manipulate your partner. (Carol thinks she has to take care of Joe.)

- Habitually feel tired, anxious, fearful, responsible, overworked and/or resentful in your relationship. (Carol feels overloaded frequently)
- Focus more on your partner's feelings, problems, circumstances, performance, satisfaction or happiness than on your own. (Rose is so concerned that John be content that she allowed herself to slide into depression without noticing)
- Feel let down, resentful, ripped off, rejected, cheated, depressed, disappointed, or otherwise dissatisfied by your partner. (Dale resents Don because he has allowed Don to overpower him in arguments)

If you have checked one or more of the above statements, you probably rescue. The more familiar these feelings or actions are, the more frequently they occur, the stronger the habit you have of rescuing in your relationship.

The second part of the checklist is to determine if you often are rescued by your partner. Again, check the statements that apply to you.

You are being rescued if you:

- Believe you are not as capable, grown up, or self-sufficient as your partner. (Michelle struggles to feel equal to Lou)
- Find that your partner is constantly doing things supposedly for you that you haven't requested or acknowledged (or may not even know about). (Fred didn't take the class for Naomi's sake,)
- Feel guilty because your partner frequently seems to work harder, do more, or want more than you do. (Joe feels guilty that Carol works and does all the housework)
- Do not need to ask for what you want, because your partner anticipates your needs, or feel reluctant to ask because your partner will not say no if he or she doesn't want to do it. (Joe doesn't need to ask Carol, she does it anyway)
- Act or feel incapable, like a child, irresponsible, paralyzed, nagged, criticized, powerless, taken care of, or manipulated in

your relationship. (Michelle often feels like a child)

- Act or feel demanding, greedy, selfish, out of control, overemotional, lazy, worthless, pampered, spoiled, helpless, or hopeless in your relationship.

- Contribute less than 50% of the effort to any project or activity that is supposed to be mutual, (including housework, earning income, making dates and social plans, initiating sex, carrying the conversations, giving comfort and support) without an agreement that your partner's extra efforts will be specifically and adequately rewarded or compensated.

- Feel your role is to be fixed, protected, controlled, felt for, worried about, ignored, or manipulated by your partner.

- Habitually feel guilty, numb, overwhelmed, turned off, irresponsible, overlooked, misunderstood and/or hopeless in your relationship.

- Focus more on your partner's approval, criticism, faults, anger, responsibility, and power than on your own opinion of yourself.

- Feel controlled, used, manipulated, victimized, abused, oppressed, stifled, limited or otherwise dissatisfied by your partner.

If you have checked one or more of the above statements, you are probably being rescued. If the feelings and actions are very familiar and you notice them frequently, your habit is strong.

Rescuing is a habit learned early in life. It seems normal, and you have done for a long time, so it may be hard to see. Rescues are secret expectations of what you should do, instead of what your partner should do. The antidote for rescuing is to give or deny permission, because you then have an open agreement, which can be renegotiated if necessary. When you learn to recognize a rescue while you are doing it your unconscious behavior becomes conscious.

Exercise: How to Stop Rescuing and/or Being Rescued

This will help you reflect on your past experience and find the clues that will alert you to the next time you are tempted to rescue.

Step 1. Recognize a Rescue While You Are Participating In It.

Part 1. To stop rescuing:

Review your relationship history, and choose a time when you felt the indicators on the rescuer checklist. Write a brief description of the events that were happening then, and answer the following questions in your description.

5.   What were the circumstances?

6.   What were you doing (or not doing)?

7.   What was your partner doing (or not doing)?

8.   Was there a discussion? If so, what did you say (or not say); what did your partner say (or not say)?

9.   Did you have an internal dialogue with yourself at the time? What was it about?

10. What was going on just before the rescue happened?

11. What led you to believe you needed to rescue your partner?

12. How did you feel about rescuing him or her?

13. How did you feel afterward?

14. What could you have done, said or perceived differently?

Whenever you realize you are rescuing, tell your partner what you want to do, and ask if they would like that or not. Once you've offered and the offer has been accepted or rejected, (even if your partner is not honest about what he or she wants, or makes a mistake) it is no longer a rescue, it is an open agreement, and can be renegotiated if necessary.

Part 2. To stop being rescued:

Review your relationship history, and choose a time when you felt the indicators on the rescued checklist. Write a description of the events that were happening then, and answer the following questions in your description.

1. What were the circumstances?
2. What were you doing (or not doing)?
3. What was your partner doing (or not doing)?
4. Was there a discussion? If so, what did you say (or not say); what did your partner say (or not say)?
5. Did you have an internal dialogue with yourself at the time? What was it about?
6. What was going on just before the rescue happened?
7. What led you to believe you needed to rescue your partner?
8. How did you feel about rescuing him or her?
9. How did you feel afterward?
10. What could you have done, said or perceived differently?
11. Whenever you realize you are being rescued, tell your partner you don't need that done for you, and suggest negotiating or talking about it. ("Don, I know you feel obligated to cook dinner for me, but actually, I would like to get my own dinner sometimes, or even cook for you. Can we talk about it?") Or, if you like being cared for just change the rescue to an open agreement by saying thank you and asking if it's truly OK.

Repeat until you are as familiar as possible with the thoughts, actions and feelings that indicate you are involved in one side or the other of a rescue.

At this point, it will be obvious when a rescue is in progress. Fixing them is quite simple.

Step 2. What to do when you are rescuing or being rescued:

Part 1. Stop, think, and report:

Whenever you notice the cues from the rescuer and rescued checklists in Step One, stop in the middle of your interaction, and ask for a moment to think about whether you're rescuing or being rescued, and what clues you are aware of. Tell your partner what you have observed, how you feel, and what you think happened. "I think I rescued you when I agreed to do all the yard maintenance last week, because I feel resentful and I don't want to do it" or, "I want to change my mind about agreeing to do the dishes every night. It feels unfair."

Part 2. *If you're unclear, review this checklist:*

If you sense there are symptoms of rescuing, but you're not clear what they are or what they mean, you can ask for a moment to think about it, and review the following checklist:

1. Are you putting out more or less than your share of the effort?
2. Are you reluctant to say what you want?
3. Are you wondering if your partner is honest about what he or she wants?
4. Do you feel uncomfortable about the interaction you and your partner are having?
5. Do you feel unsatisfied with the result?
6. Are you trying to keep your partner from being hurt, angry, upset, sad, or disappointed?
7. Does this feel similar to interactions you've had before, where you felt bad at the end?

The more yes answers you have, the more likely that you are involved in rescuing or being rescued at this moment. If you answered no to all of these questions, you are probably not involved in a rescue.

Step 3. Propose to negotiate:

Tell your partner that you feel uncomfortable with the interaction between you, and what clues you perceive; and ask if he or she is uncomfortable too. Discuss what either of you are doing that you feel resentful or unhappy about and ask your partner if he or she will negotiate with you.

Carol asked to negotiate new housecleaning arrangements and Joe volunteered to take over, even though he didn't want to. At first, Joe felt noble for helping Carol, but he soon realized he was feeling resentful, burdened, and that he was avoiding doing what he promised. Those feelings were his clue that he probably rescued Carol (Checklist, and step 1.) He thought about the situation and realized that although he was fully understanding and supportive of Carol when it came to her feeling overworked and uncared for, he had a similar problem. He realized that he hadn't considered his own needs when he offered to do the housework (Step 2). At that point, he went to Carol and proposed to negotiate their housekeeping situation so that both of their needs could be met, using step 3.

Even though you want to give up rescuing or being rescued, your partner may not. If that happens, treat rescuing as a refusal to negotiate, and use the Trouble Shooting Guide (Chapter 6) to overcome it. Even if your partner persists in rescuing or wanting to be rescued, if you state out loud what you believe is going on, you turn the rescue into an open agreement, and open agreements can be discussed and negotiated.

Gentle Persistence

Sometimes, no matter how good you are at communication techniques, how clearly you've defined the problem, or how carefully you've asked for an agreement to negotiate, your partner will still refuse. This can happen whether you're brand new at negotiating, or even on occasion after you have had several successful negotiations where both of you were completely happy with the results.

There are a lot of possible reasons why your partner (or you) could be reluctant or unwilling to negotiate:

- If your partner is suspicious of the process,
- If the problem is particularly scary to either of you,
- If one of you is afraid of being manipulated or over powered,
- If the problem seems insurmountable,
- If one of you is accustomed to being in charge,
- If the problem involves a life change.

If, for any reason you have tried all the techniques in this chapter and your partner still refuses to negotiate, don't give up! If you've tried everything you can think of, and your partner still won't agree to negotiate, gentle persistence is what you need.

Gentle persistence is the art of staying focused on your objective (solving your problem, getting an agreement to negotiate) and repeatedly asking your partner to participate, without sounding critical, impatient, pushy, overbearing or dictatorial. Gentle persistence can be a very effective and valuable skill for getting an agreement to negotiate.

Most of us only know how to persist in a nagging, complaining, whining or angry way; all styles based in the belief that the other person won't cooperate, and has to be made unhappy or uncomfortable enough to give in. Gentle persistence is based on a belief that your partner is a reasonable person who wants to cooperate, but somehow (even after all your communicating, I messages, and invitations to negotiate) hasn't heard you, misinterprets or doesn't understand that's what you want.

Here's how Rose used Gentle Persistence to get John to listen to her:

Rose: John, I want to talk to you.

John: (offhand) Sure, go ahead; I've always got time to listen to the little woman.

Rose: (stating problem) John, I want to get a job and I want both of us to work out a way for both of us to be comfortable with that.

John: (not believing) Oh, Rose, you're not serious. What do you want, more money or new clothes?

Rose: (still calm, explains more) No, John, I want to get a job. I want to get out of the house and meet people. I want to have a career. Can we discuss it?

John: (trying to distract her) Now, now, Rose. Why don't we just go out to dinner tonight?

Rose: (still calm, more definite) John, please listen to me. I'm serious.

John: (looking for an excuse) Is it your time of the month? You seem upset.

Rose: (still calm, firmer) I am not having emotional, physical or mental problems. I have made a decision about my life, and that involves you. I want your cooperation. I want you to know I am firm about this and I will keep bringing it up until you agree to discuss the matter with me like two adults.

John: (she got his attention with that, but he's skeptical) Gee, I guess you are serious. But how can you mean it? VanDerGelder women have never worked: my mother took pride in her house and children; she didn't need to work.

Rose: (reassuring, still firm) John, your mother was a fine woman. And so am I. These are different times. I want a new challenge. I know we can get your needs taken care of, too. A maid can keep house, and the children are grown. They don't need me. I need to feel productive again.

John: (opening up, sharing fears) But, Rose, what will my business associates think? What about our position? Who will take care of me?

Rose: (reassuring, more gentle persistence) I don't want to discomfort or embarrass you. Let's sit down and discuss it, and I'm sure we can work it out. We're both intelligent and creative. A solution that pleases both of us can't be too hard to find.

John: (agrees) Well, all right. I don't like it, but I'm willing to discuss it.

Even though John is very reluctant even to consider Rose's request serious, her gentle persistence brought him around at least to a willingness to try. Such persistence may need to be repeated over a period of days or weeks, if your partner is very reluctant to listen or has a difficult time understanding what you mean, but, if you can resist the impulse to nag or complain, you will be successful.

When you gently persist, like Rose:
- You let your partner know that the problem you're experiencing is very important and must be resolved, but in a gentle, uncritical, non-threatening way.
- You gently but firmly refuse to give up your power to create good things in your life together, just because one of you is scared, angry or stubborn.

- You stay focused on your purpose, and don't let yourself be drawn off course.
- You calmly and lovingly refuse to take no for an answer.

Gentle persistence is not as hard as it may sound, and once you try it, you will be very motivated to do it, because it works. The reward for gently persisting is an agreement to negotiate, a mutually satisfactory solution, and a relationship that works for both of you.

The following guidelines will support your effort and help you keep your persistence from becoming pushy or manipulative.

Guidelines for Gentle Persistence

1) Be well prepared before trying gentle persistence:

Gentle persistence requires that you be in firm control of yourself. Choose a moment when you feel strong, and you and your partner have some peaceful, uninterrupted time. You are demonstrating adult, thoughtful, calm and rational interaction for your partner, even if your partner is aggravating, dismissive or childish in his or her responses, so you must feel strong and comfortable enough to stay calm and positive in the face of negative responses. Be sure you're not upset, exhausted, fearful or angry when you try it. That means you may need to take care of yourself by blowing off steam elsewhere (in writing, to a friend) if you get annoyed, or dropping the subject temporarily (and coming back later) because you've run out of patience.

Until your partner realizes the importance of cooperative negotiation in general, or the importance of this particular issue to you, you are in the role of educator. Know clearly what your goal is (to get an agreement to negotiate about your problem) and that you're willing to explain it as many times as necessary, remaining calm every time.

Rose chose a time when she felt strong and calm and waited until she was clear enough (using Problem Inventory, Chapter 3) about what she wanted to persist with John, and she successfully remained calm even when he seemed to belittle her.

2. You both deserve to have what you want:

Gentle persistence is based on the conviction that you and your partner both deserve to get what you want. You're not asking for permission to have your way. You're making a firm offer to your partner to participate in the process and be satisfied also. You won't feel guilty, helpless, hopeless or angry when you hold that point of view. You're working to create a change (from competing or rescuing to cooperation) that is beneficial to both of you and your relationship, and even raises the odds that your relationship will continue to be successful. Rose's conviction that she is doing something good and necessary for both of them shows in her statement "John, I want to get a job and I want both of us to work out a way for both of us to be comfortable with that."

3. Be gentle and firm:

Gentleness means treating your partner with respect and caring, while firmness means not giving in or giving up. If your partner says something, listen and answer it (with reassurance or I statements), but don't agree unless it's meeting your objective. Don't slide into nagging, manipulating, pushing, coercing, or abusing. Let your partner know that the issue is important to you, that you are serious about finding a satisfactory solution, that you want his or her participation in solving it, and you're not going to give up or forget the idea. Rose used firm words: "I want", "I've made a decision" -- she did not say, "would you like to...","I think I want...", "maybe..." or "would you be angry if I...".

4. Be sincere about cooperating:

Before you try gentle persistence; be sure you really are willing to negotiate and that you honestly want your partner to be satisfied, too, so that your invitation to your partner to participate is genuine.

If you desire a cooperative, equal relationship, and your partner doesn't understand the value of that, it's up to you to lead the way; so you must accept the responsibility of being cooperative whether or not your partner agrees to participate. No matter what attempts John made to put Rose off or distract or annoy her, she didn't lose sight of her objective, get angry, or disparage him.

5. Seek to understand your partner's resistance:

Any or all of the barriers (Inexperience and Mistrust, The Power Struggle Habit, or Rescuing) can be in the way. Use active listening and attentive speaking to encourage your partner to talk about his or her reluctance, and review the sections in this chapter on the barriers. Rose used I messages frequently, and reassured John whenever she he expressed a concern.

6. Be as objective as possible:

When you express what you feel, use I messages, and don't expect your partner to agree. Instead, try to see both sides: why you want to negotiate, as well as why your partner doesn't. The better you understand your partner's attitude and concerns, the more effective you will be at reassuring and convincing him or her that agreeing to negotiate will benefit both of you. Seek to explain the benefits of negotiating as your partner would perceive them, through reassurance and active listening.

Rose's statements "your mother was a fine woman." and "I know we can get your needs taken care of, too." were responses to hearing John's point of view.

7. Address your partner's fear:

You may need to reassure your partner many times while you are gently persisting, because you are changing the rules for how you deal with each other, which is unsettling and produces anxiety. Unwillingness to negotiate almost always indicates fear of the outcome. It can be very reassuring to remind your partner, as Rose did: "I don't want to discomfort or embarrass you." or our basic, "I want both of us to be satisfied. I won't consider this negotiation successful or complete unless you get what you want, too."

8. Remind your partner of your good will:

Love and respect usually reduce defensiveness and make cooperation easier. Take some time to remind yourself of all the good and valuable aspects of your relationship, and then share them with your partner. Tell your partner you believe that together, you can solve the problem. There is a further discussion of good will and how to establish it in the next chapter, Setting the Stage.

Rose expressed her good will at the end: "I'm sure we can work it out. We're both intelligent and creative. A solution that pleases both of us can't be too hard to find."

With all the powerful techniques and guidelines you have learned about so far, chances are you will have gotten an agreement to negotiate by this time, and be ready to move on to the next step, Setting the Stage (Chapter Five). But, in those rare cases where all the previous techniques have still not resulted in an agreement to negotiate, there are still some powerful remedies to try. The following Trouble Shooting Guide will help you figure out why your attempt to get an Agreement didn't work, and tell you what to do about it.

Exercise: Trouble Shooting Guide

This guide is intended to help you figure out what techniques to use if you've tried everything you can think of, but you're still stuck and cannot get an agreement to negotiate. The Trouble Shooting Guide will help you any time you are unable to proceed or figure out why. It will help you pinpoint how and why you are not getting an agreement to negotiate, and remind you of what to do about it. Use it the same way you'd use a trouble shooting manual for new technology.

Problem: Your partner doesn't understand what cooperative problem solving is, or doesn't trust that it will work:

If only you have read this book, your partner may not know what is expected or intended. If your partner is interested in reading *How to Be Happy Partners,* you can discuss it together. If not, you can explain cooperative negotiating in your own words, why it is important to you, and what about it is different from the way you usually handle problems. (Use Effective Communication Guidelines and Guidelines for Reassurance in Chapter 3)

Once your partner understands what you are proposing and agrees that it is worth trying, you can show the negotiation tree, and try again to define the problem and ask for an agreement to negotiate.

Problem: You try to get an agreement to negotiate and end up arguing.

Did you ask for an agreement to negotiate in a way that your partner can understand? Find out what your partner is thinking. Listen to your partner's concerns as well as explaining yours. The more you care about and respect your partner's feelings and opinions, the more likely it is that yours will be heard. Use the simplest possible way to: 1) give information, 2) use attentive speaking (Chapter 3), and 3) Listen and play back what you hear, so you both know you understand each other.

Problem: You believe your partner understands your intentions, but still won't agree.

Your partner may not trust that you can work together to get what both of you want, and you may need to resolve these fears. Or your partner may fear that you will argue and damage your relationship. Respect your partner's fears, and reassure that you care too much to hurt, cheat, or degrade your partner because you care about their feelings, wants and needs, too. Reminding yourself and your partner that a negotiation is not cooperative unless both of you are satisfied with the result can make a lot of the anxiety and fear go away, and create an atmosphere where negotiation is much easier. The specific reassurance to give will vary with the kind of fear being experienced.

If you think your partner is worried, anxious or afraid, ask what the fear is about: "Are you worried about something?" "You seem reluctant to work with me on this. Will you tell me why?"

Once you understand the fears, you can directly reassure your partner: "No, I'm not trying to talk you into something you don't want to do. I care about your feelings, too, and I also care about mine. I'm trying to find a way we can work together so we can both get what we want." Or, "No, we won't struggle about this all night. Let's try it for an hour, and if we haven't got it solved by then, we'll make a new date to try it again. We don't even have to do it right now. I'm just asking if you're willing to solve the problem with me. We can figure out a time to do it later." (See "Overcoming the Power Struggle Habit")

Problem: You've tried all the other suggestions and still can't agree to negotiate:

Even if you've followed steps one, two and three of this trouble shooting guide, and read through and applied everything in the chapter, and your partner is still unwilling, don't give up. Persistence is often the key to successful negotiation. For now, take a break and drop the subject to give your partner time to think about it. You can gently bring it up later which usually works very well. Your partner's initial resistance may be a result of feeling rushed or pushed, and needing some time to think about it before making an agreement. (See Gentle Persistence)

Problem: Even gentle persistence doesn't work:

When all else fails, the cooperative thing to do is to solve the problem yourself, inform your partner what your solution is, let him or her know you'd rather solve it together, and leave an open invitation for your partner to join you in cooperatively solving the problem at any time. Solving the problem to your own satisfaction, no matter what your partner may want, creates a great incentive for him or her to join you in negotiating, where his or her wants will be considered, too. The following section on Solving it Yourself will help you do this more effectively.

Here's how Carol, using the Trouble Shooting Guide, persuades Joe to learn about and try cooperative problem solving:

Carol: (communicating clearly and inviting him to learn more about negotiation) Joe, I'm reading about cooperative problem solving as a way to designing our relationship so it totally suits us both. It's about how we can learn to work together better, so we can both be more satisfied and happy together. I'm really excited about it, and I'd like to try it out. Does it sound interesting to you?

Joe: (not enthused, wary) I don't know. What would I have to do?

Carol: (offering options, reassuring) Well, either you could read this book like I did, I could read it aloud, or I could explain it to you as I understand it.

114

Joe: (more interested, still not sure) Sounds interesting, but do we need it? Aren't we doing fine already?

Carol: (communicating, persisting, reassuring) I think you would like some things you are not getting and this is a way for you to get more of what you want. There are also a few important wrinkles for me that we need to iron out and I think this might help us do that.

Joe: (cautiously considering it) OK, as long as you aren't expecting too much. I don't want to feel pressured to make a lot of changes because of some book, but I am willing to read it, if you give me a couple of weeks.

-- *two weeks later* --

Carol: (gently persisting) Well, I know you read the book. What do you think?

Joe: (still not convinced) It sounds too good to be true, and also like a lot of work and I don't know if it's worth it.

Carol: (persisting, reassuring) Joe, if it works, it'll be worth it, won't it? Remember my problem about housework? And I know you're not getting all the sexual contact you want. Maybe this will help us work those things out.

Joe: (seeing some advantages to CPS) I see what you mean, but it still sounds too good to be true.

Carol: (persisting, saying she'll solve it for herself) Let's try it just a couple of times, and if it won't work, maybe we'll try counseling or something else. I do think our problems aren't going to go away; they'll just get worse if we don't do something. If we don't try this, and you won't go to counseling, I'll have to go by myself, and work on it alone. You won't be participating, so you might not like the result. This, on the other hand, is focused on getting you what you want, too. Why not try it?

Joe: (recognizing he could lose out if he doesn't try) OK, when you put it that way, I guess it's worth a try.

Once you have an agreement to negotiate, you are past the most difficult part of cooperative problem solving. The next step is Setting the Stage, where you will learn to set up and maintain an atmosphere that keeps your negotiation in a relaxed, positive, non-confrontational attitude of cooperation. But, what do you do after you have tried everything and your partner still won't agree to negotiate?

Solve it for Yourself

You may believe you have only two options if your partner won't agree to negotiate:

1. You can attempt to pressure or convince your partner to change: you can push, nag, badger, pressure, whine, complain, reason, yell, resist, pout or physically abuse your partner. Or,

2. You can give up: walk out, sacrifice, submit, comply, withdraw, withhold or accept your partner's decision. You may not realize the third option: You can choose to come up with a solution that makes you happy.

We call this Solving the Problem for Yourself.

If you are faced with a partner who won't or can't negotiate with you, solving the problem for yourself bypasses all the struggle, hassle and arguing, and goes straight to solving the problem. It is the most powerful encouragement for your partner to join in and agree to negotiate, because your partner does not get to help choose the solution unless you both participate. This is not done in a spirit of "OK, you won't negotiate, so I'll show you." but in a spirit of "I understand that you don't want discuss this, so I'll have to solve it for myself, as best I can. When you are ready to cooperate and negotiate, I'll be available."

There are several benefits to this approach:

- It is liberating to realize that you don't have to have your partner's participation to be satisfied.
- You also don't have to shut your partner out or be unkind.
- You no longer have the problem you were concerned about.
- You can still have a good, loving, relationship, because you have not done anything bad to your partner (if he or she doesn't like your solution, he or she can negotiate), and you

aren't feeling frustrated, angry and deprived.

- It takes the pressure off your partner, who is likely to relax and be less defensive or more interested.
- It prevents you from being helpless and frustrated, so you can welcome your partner's cooperation when he or she offers it.

To solve the problem alone, you need to believe you are entitled to satisfaction. Caring about your partner's wants and needs (as well as your own) is central to cooperation, but you cannot effectively meet your partner's needs without his or her help. Therefore, when your partner refuses to negotiate, he or she leaves you no choice but to focus on your own need until he or she agrees to participate.

As long as you offer every opportunity to cooperate and you extend an invitation to your partner to work with you at any time, you are free to solve the problem for yourself. You don't need to rescue and try to please your partner at your own expense, because if you neither of you can be satisfied. Solving it for yourself puts you in control of your wellbeing and ends waiting for your partner to cooperate.

Joe has stored up a lot of frustration, because Carol has been late too many times, so he's decided to try solving the problem for himself:

Joe: (angry, but calm) I've been standing here waiting for you for 45 minutes. You said you'd be here at 6:00. Carol, this happens too much and it's not acceptable to me anymore. I've tried to get you to talk about it with me, and you never want to.

Carol: (sheepish, not too concerned) I'm sorry. One thing led to another and I lost track of time.

Joe: (determined) I've heard that too many times before! I am not willing to be stood up like this again. It's too late tonight, the movie's already started, so let's go out for a bite to eat, and I'll tell you what I've decided about this.

Carol: OK.

-- at a coffee shop, a little later --

Joe: (persisting) I said I'd tell you what I've decided about being late, so here it is.

Carol: (trying to change subject) Ah, Joe...

Joe: (persisting) No, please don't interrupt me. You need to hear this, because it will affect you.

Carol: (agreeing to listen) OK.

Joe: (firmly and clearly) I don't want to be left waiting again. From now on when we make plans, I will wait for fifteen minutes, max. If you are not there in that time, I'll leave, so I don't have to get angry. If you call before our scheduled time and say you'll be late, and it's OK with me, we can negotiate about how long I'll wait. If we're going to a party or a show, I will leave a note and your ticket if any, and you can join me when you get there, but I don't want to miss any more opening numbers or be late to any more movies because I'm waiting for you.

Joe: (continuing) Also, I won't make plans to meet you anywhere where I will be embarrassed or uncomfortable if you're late, such as having to sit around a restaurant, wondering if you'll show up. Either we can go to the restaurant together, or we can invite someone else along, so I have someone to sit with if you are late. This way, I won't be angry, and we won't have to fight any more. On my part, I will be clear about when your being on time is important to me, and when timing is not so important, I will not be unreasonable about it. If I'm just puttering about at home, and you're late, that's really not a problem, and I won't turn it in to one.

Carol: (unhappy) Gee, Joe, it sounds pretty strict.

Joe: (standing firm, but explaining and reassuring) It has to be, Carol, or I'll get so angry I won't see you anymore, and there's too much that's good about this relationship to let a simple thing like this mess it up. I love you, but I just can't wait around anymore. It makes me feel unloved and uncared about, and that's not fair, because in many other ways, I know you love me.

Carol: (resisting) What if I don't agree?

Joe: (offering to negotiate) We can work out another solution together, that makes both of us happy.

Carol: (thinking about it) Maybe that's a good idea. Let's make a time to discuss it.

Sometimes, problems are more serious, and solving it yourself is necessary to protect yourself, as it is with Carla and Ann. Carla, in the following example, is frustrated about the way her partner Ann deals with money, to the point that Carla's credit and financial security are being jeopardized. This is an issue that creates problems for many couples.

Carla: (concerned) You haven't been contributing to our household account lately. You already owe me money from the past, and for three weeks, I've bought the groceries and paid this month's gas and water bills. Are you in financial trouble again?

Ann: (offhand) I've had some expenses. I'll get caught up on pay day.

Carla: (not accepting that answer, persisting) Your half of the current expenses so far is $185 and I'll need money for next month in the account: that's another $200 plus the rent.

Ann: (still unconcerned) OK.

--*after payday* --

Carla: (persisting) Do you have the money for the household account?

Ann: (casual) I'm a little short. Here's $100 and I'll catch the rest up later.

Carla: (not going along) I'm feeling used here. I want you to pay your share and you're not. I want to talk this out and get this problem solved.

Ann: (denying) Look, there's no problem. I'll be all caught up next week.

Carla: (persisting) Ann, I've heard that before. I have a problem with how we handle money together, and I want to work it out with you.

Ann: (getting defensive) I told you not to worry about it. I'll take care of it next week. Now, leave me alone.

Carla: (realizing she's not getting cooperation, asking for negotiation) You don't seem to understand that I'm feeling really bad about this. I love you a lot and I'm worried about our relationship. How can we be together if you're not paying for your half? I don't earn enough for both of us, and even if I did, it isn't fair. Let's sit down tonight and work this out. This is very serious.

Ann: (refusing, changing subject) Will you please just relax? Let's go out and lighten up. I'll treat for a movie tonight.

Later, after pondering the whole situation, Carla decides it's serious enough that she has to solve it for herself. She decides to resort to a tough solution. In the midst of her emotional turmoil, Carla doesn't trust herself to be clear and calm in conversation with Ann, nor did she think Ann would take her seriously unless she wrote it down, so Carla writes the following letter, which is a good way to be sure Ann has a chance to understand Carla's unilateral decision:

Dear Ann:

As you probably realize, I am very unhappy with our current financial dealings. I don't seem to be able to find a way to get you to see how important it is to me that you pay your share of expenses, on time and without being reminded. I've attempted to discuss this with you, with no success. So, I've made a decision on my own. I've thought this through very carefully, and I want you to know how very much I love you. I am very sad and frustrated because I can't find a way to encourage you to help me reach a solution that will work for both of us.

I've decided to solve the problem as best I can without you and here's my solution:

- I'm only going to buy food for myself. I won't share it with you until we work the problem out.

- You have a good job, and you make enough money to live on. I don't know what's wrong, because you won't tell me, but your lateness on bills and the rent is beginning to ruin my credit, and I'm no longer going to pay your share. I'm giving you thirty days' notice that if you don't pay your share of the expenses and the rent, we'll use the last month's rent we have coming next month, and I'll move out. I hate doing this, because I like living with you, but it seems like the only way to protect myself from your money problems.

- If that happens, I would still like to see you, and be your partner, but without the financial entanglements.

I want us both to be happy and be able to stay together, so if you want to work this out some other way, and pay your full share, or at least tell me the truth about what's wrong, I'm more than willing to help. If you have a suggestion about how you can get what you want and I can still feel financially secure, I'd be happy to discuss it, but I can't accept any more empty promises. I just am not willing to feel used and taken advantage of anymore. It's damaging my feelings for you.

With much love and some anger, Carla

In the letter, Carla has taken a stand on behalf of herself, and what she believes is her only chance for a satisfying life with Ann. Carla's solution is drastic, but very effective at releasing her from problems being caused by Ann. She knows that if this money issue goes on any longer, her good feelings about Ann will be destroyed, and so would their relationship. Carla has now regained control of her financial wellbeing and still left an open invitation to Ann to continue the rest of the relationship and even to renegotiate their financial arrangement on a more honest and realistic basis. Ann still has choices, but she no longer can put Carla in financial jeopardy.

Ann makes enough money to support herself, so her nonpayment is evidence that this could be a serious problem that requires a strong, tough solution. Even though Carla is horrified at the thought of losing Ann, she isn't willing to sacrifice herself and allow Ann's financial problem (and Carla's anger) to get worse.

This letter has an excellent chance of getting Ann's attention, and achieving Carla's true goal, which is to work together on the problem. If Ann still won't negotiate, her problem is severe, and Carla truly needs to protect herself by separating her funds from Ann's. At this point, Carla must allow Ann to make up her mind about what she wants to do. By putting their relationship on the line, while also continuing to offer to negotiate, Carla is presenting the strongest possible motivation for Ann to want to deal with the problem, and also protecting herself in case Ann is so out of control that she can't fix it.

If your problem is not as serious as Ann and Carla's, then your solution will be much less drastic, like Joe's, but the attitude of taking care of yourself while leaving the offer to negotiate open is the same.

In solving this serious problem for themselves with their separate partners, Carla and Joe followed several steps. By following the same steps, you can be sure you've given your partner ample opportunity to cooperate, and you're not overreacting:

Guidelines for Solving It Yourself

1. Make sure you've made a thorough attempt to negotiate:

- Have you Defined the Problem, using all the techniques in Chapter Five? (Problem Inventory, Creating Permission, Analyzing Rights and Responsibilities, and Discovering Secret Expectations)?
- Have you used all the techniques and skills in this chapter in asking for an Agreement to Negotiate (Overcoming Inexperience and Mistrust, Communicating Clearly, Reassurance, and Gentle Persistence)?

To cover these steps, Carla opens her letter with a review of the problem and statements that she's tried to negotiate it. Review the problem and your attempts to solve it before telling your partner that you're solving it yourself. You can then open your discussion or letter with these facts.

2. Tell your partner what you are doing:

State clearly that you have attempted to negotiate the problem, that your assessment is that your partner doesn't want to work on it, that you would prefer to work on it together, but that you've decided what you are going to do about it on your own. Carla writes how sad she is to have to resort to such a stern solution; Joe explains that he's protecting what's good about the relationship.

3. Invite your partner to negotiate at any time:

Say that you are going to follow your own solution unless your partner wants to discuss it, but that you are open to discussing it at any time if it makes him or her unhappy. This is your open invitation to negotiate at any time; which makes the difference between an ultimatum and a negotiating strategy. It keeps the attitude of cooperation intact.

3. Communicate your good will:

Let your partner know that you value him or her and the partnership, and you don't like having to make unilateral decisions, but you feel you have no choice, because you can't force him or her to work on it with you. Carla said how much she loved Ann, and how she hated to do this, and Joe says he wants to protect his good feelings for Carol.

4. Be Sure Your Solution Solves the Problem for You:

Using the Guidelines for Sharing Wants (Chapter 5) and Brainstorming (Chapter 6) exercises, find a solution that solves the problem in a way that's satisfying for you, even if you think your partner may not like it. If the solution works for both of you, the problem is solved, and needs no further discussion. If your partner is not satisfied with your solution, he or she has already been invited to negotiate; making your own choice is a powerful incentive.

A good rule of thumb in finding your own solution is to imagine what you would do about the problem if your partner weren't part of it. What would you do if your best friend were involved? Would it be different? Would the problem change if you lived alone or were single? What would you do then?

Considering a relationship problem from the vantage point of a single person often points out places where you're being needlessly dependent. Because she was in financial jeopardy through her partner's refusal to cooperate, Carla's solution was to get financially untangled from Ann, while hoping to keep the emotional connection.

If Ann does genuinely care, and is not just using Carla for financial support, this decision will get her attention, and get her interested in solving the problem. If not, Carla is at least saving herself from a disastrous financial situation.

Before Carla made the decision, Ann's irresponsible behavior was Carla's problem. Now, it has become Ann's problem. Joe's problem is less severe, because it is just an inconvenience, but it still adversely affected his feelings for Carol. Joe's solution eliminates his feeling of powerlessness and not being cared about, and allows Carol's problem with lateness to affect only her.

In obtaining an agreement to negotiate, you have learned:

- to communicate what you want, and how problem solving works,
- to reassure and encourage your partner to participate; to persist gently, until your partner understands how important it is to you;
- to overcome inexperience and mistrust by using the Trouble Shooting Guidelines,
- to turn power struggles into cooperation,
- to change old habits of rescuing and resenting the result, and, if all else fails,
- to solve the problem yourself to demonstrate a solution and motivate your partner to be part a negotiation.

Hopefully, you will seldom need to solve a problem without your partner's cooperation, but knowing you can solve the problem for yourself and still be willing to negotiate with your partner means you can remain calm; which is much for your relationship than feeling frustrated, angry and ripped off. In the next chapter, you will learn the next steps of Cooperative Problem and how to begin the actual negotiation.

Chapter Four

Set the Stage

Once you've learned Defining the Problem and Agreeing to Negotiate, the hardest steps of The Negotiation Tree, you are on your way to establishing equal partnership, teamwork and cooperation via negotiation. In setting the stage, you'll create an atmosphere and attitude which will support cooperation and successful problem solving.

While it takes a whole chapter to fully explain and to teach you the skills you need, you'll find in actual practice setting the stage usually takes only moments.

There are four parts:

1. *choose the time and place,*
2. *establish goodwill,*
3. *reassure each other, and*
4. *set aside held anger and hurt.*

When you and your partner rush into problem solving too quickly, you can feel harried, confused, angry and/or trapped in negotiating because you haven't created the time, the energy or the good will (motivation) to carry on. The resulting tension can sidetrack your negotiation and impede all the progress you've made in defining the problem and agreeing to negotiate, especially if you and your partner are inexperienced or are negotiating a particularly difficult or long-standing problem.

When you and your partner realize there is a problem, you may agree to solve it together, but you pick a time when you feel rushed or tired, or pick an inappropriate setting that is uncomfortable, or not private enough. Or, you can be too vague about where and when, and the discussion never happens. The bigger the problem, the more important setting a time and place becomes.

Choosing time and place

When you both agree to reserve time to negotiate calmly and be relaxed you'll have better chance of success. Choose a time when you both are rested and relaxed and you won't be rushed or interrupted; it will allow you the time you need to think clearly and to explore all the aspects of the problem. Uninterrupted time will allow you to solve the problem as quickly and efficiently as possible, and reduce tension between you. In addition to creating enough time and a good setting for uninterrupted negotiating, choosing the time and place also helps you establish the emotional climate of mutual caring and teamwork that is essential to your success. Without it you are less likely to work together cooperatively.

Rose, after figuring out how to define the problem, and getting John's agreement to negotiate, agrees to put off the discussion until later, because John has work he brought home from the office. Days pass, and nothing more is said. Rose, who struggled to bring up the problem in the first place, feels reluctant to broach the subject again, but finally she does.

Rose: (hesitantly) John, do you remember when I said I had a problem about the children being gone and not having enough to do?

John: (reading papers) Uh-huh.

Rose: (without much hope) You said you'd discuss it with me.

John: (distracted) Not now, dear, I'm tired.

Rose: (disappointed) OK. (gives up.)

   -- the next morning --

Rose: (quietly fuming) John, you said you'd discuss the problem with me, and I want to talk about it now.

John: (rushed) Rose, don't pester me before work. You know I have to catch my train. I don't have time now.

Rose: (angry) Work, work, work! It's all you ever think about. You never want to talk about my important issues. You love your work more than you love me.

John: (angry, too) Ok, I've had it! Don't you dare complain about my work. I've earned a good living for you and the children all these years. Just leave me alone. (Grabs coat and briefcase leaves and slams the door.)

Rose and John have just wiped out all the progress they made on the first two steps, and now they're both angry because neither of them realized how important choosing a time and place was. Rose picked a time when John was tired, and he didn't realize that she was trying to reopen the negotiation. Then, because she was frustrated at his lack of response, she became impatient and anxious, and tried to insist on negotiating at a time when John had to catch a train.

He felt badgered and trapped, and responded by getting angry and leaving. They had an agreement to negotiate, but they had not chosen a time and place that was agreeable to both of them.

However, once they learn to use this step of The Negotiation Tree, they are more thoughtful about when and where they negotiate:

Rose: John, do you remember when I said I had a problem about the children being gone and not having enough to do?

John: (reading the paper) Uh-huh. (Puts down paper, thinks a minute) Oh, yes. We agreed to negotiate. When do you want to do it?

Rose: (considering time and place) I know you're tired now, and it wouldn't go very well. What about having a nice dinner at home tomorrow night, and then sitting down to talk afterwards?

John: That sounds good. (agreeing on time and place) I'll make sure I'm home by 6:00. Will that work?

Rose: (Agrees) Thank you. I really appreciate your cooperation. I'll make your favorite dinner: pot roast and noodles.

John: (satisfied) It will be a pleasure. We need a good, long talk and some time together. (He goes back to his paper. Rose, reassured, picks up a book). What Rose and John have done is to choose the time and place of their negotiation.

The following steps will help you choose a time and place more effectively.

Exercise: Choosing Time and Place

1. Evaluate problem for time needed:

Consider the problem you are negotiating: Has it been long-standing? Does it seem that you are on opposite sides and will never agree? Are you able to think of several possible solutions, or are you locked into just one outcome?

The more difficult the problem seems, and the more insistent either of you is on a certain outcome, the longer it will probably take to solve. The more relaxed you are, and the more extended time you have, the more likely it is that the problem will be easily solved. So, when you have a difficult problem, choose a time and place that is open-ended, or decide in advance that the negotiation may take more than one session. When you're new at cooperative problem solving, allow more time than you think you need. As you become more familiar with the process your estimates of the time you need will become more accurate.

2. Consider both your schedules:

Many couples have different schedules and preferences. One of you may be more alert and better-natured in the AM, and the other more apt to be effective in the evening.

Both of you may be busier on weekends (for example, with kids, laundry, shopping, etc.) and more relaxed on weeknights after work. Or, your work schedules might conflict. Compare your schedules, and select a time that works well for both of you. If one of you is more stressed about the problem, choose a time that makes it easiest for that partner. After trying a few negotiation sessions at different times, you'll find the best times for problem-solving.

3. Arrange to be uninterrupted:

When choosing the time and place, remember that it is important to be uninterrupted. Turn off phones, television and computers. Find a way to occupy the children, or ask someone to watch them for a while, and don't answer the door.

Establish Good Will

Good will between partners is a combination of the trust, affection, and positive regard the partners have toward each other. When you like and respect each other, you'll get along better because you both feel cared about, appreciated, trusted and loving. You will have an easier time working together when you and your partner establish the good will you have for each other when you start. It will remind you that solving this problem is a way to enhance the good relationship you already have. When you remember that you both desire your mutual benefit and satisfaction, you'll enjoy working together.

If you forget to establish good will you can forget to put the problem in its proper perspective to the relationship, compete with each other and regard fixing the problem as your only chance to make the relationship work, and the negotiation can degenerate into an argument.

Rose and John, before they learned to Establish Good Will, had many heated and frustrating encounters like the following:

> *(After dinner, at the agreed-upon time)*
>
> *Rose:* (abruptly, anxious, not clear) OK, John, let's discuss my problem. I'm unhappy, and I feel restless and useless. I can't go on like this.
>
> *John:* (getting tense) What do you want to do?
>
> *Rose:* (not problem solving, just reacting) I don't know. I just feel unhappy. Maybe I should get a job.

John: (back to his old ideas) Rose, you don't need to work. I make enough money. I want you here at home.

Rose: (angry) You just don't hear me. I have to do something meaningful.

John: (angry) So find something meaningful to do! Don't bother me with it! (discussion ends with both of them dissatisfied and frustrated)

After Rose and John learn the importance of establishing good will, the dialogue goes differently:

Rose: (talks about good feelings) John, I appreciate you being here to discuss this problem with me. You and I have solved a lot of problems together, and I trust your advice and judgement.

John: (lets her know he cares) Rose, I enjoyed this meal, and I'm looking forward to our discussion. You know that I have always wanted you to be happy, and I'm sure we can work this out together.

(Both are now reminded of their long, successful association, and ready to work together to solve the problem, which now feels more mutual.)

The following exercise can help you learn to express and develop your loving appreciation for yourselves, each other and your relationship.

Exercise: Establishing Good Will

The few moments it takes to establish good will, make problem solving vastly easier by reminding and reassuring both of you that you genuinely want to work together to solve this problem and to build a better relationship. Always establish good will at the beginning of a negotiation. You can also use it any time the atmosphere gets tense or you get discouraged or worried about the outcome of your discussion.

1. Review past successes:

You and your partner have had successes, even if they are hard to remember when you are struggling. Your courtship was a success, or you wouldn't be together. You have had good times and accomplished goals together. Perhaps you have children, a house or car, saved money, gone to movies or dinners, celebrated anniversaries, survived illnesses, decorated your house or apartment, enjoyed family or friends, or taken vacations or trips together. When you remind each other of these good times, you reactivate loving feelings, and are reminded of why you are together today.

A. Select three positive events

Select three positive events or successful interactions from your history, when you felt good and enjoyed being together. Go back in time as far as the first excitement of meeting each other and dating, if necessary. Think about these positive events for a few minutes, and remember them clearly enough to describe them to your partner. Write them down to help clarify them.

B.Share positive memories:

Share the memories you have collected, to remind each other how good things can be; until you feel some of those positive feelings toward each other right now and remember that you're partners who love each other before moving on to the next step.

2. Acknowledge the importance of your partnership:

Remind each other that you care about each other, or you wouldn't even be trying to work things out. You have made an investment of time, energy and caring in each other and in the relationship. Remind each other how long you've been together, and that you want to go on happily together.

3. Agree that a cooperative solution can be found:

Even if you're not sure a mutually satisfactory solution can be found, tell each other there must be a way to cooperate in this situation, and you intend to do everything you can to find what it is. Say "I want both of us to be satisfied with the solution."

Establishing good will creates the atmosphere of mutual caring, trust and teamwork that you need to feel cooperative. Even so, you may feel anxious; which requires reassurance.

Reassurance

Reassurance calms you down when you're anxious about the result of the negotiation, and reminds you that this negotiation is just about a single problem, and does not mean your whole relationship is in jeopardy. Disagreements create tension, so both you and your partner are likely to be somewhat anxious about the outcome of your negotiation.

Reassuring each other reduces this anxiety, which means you will be able to think more clearly, be less likely to overreact emotionally, and cooperate more successfully. You'll find reassurance is very useful whenever either of you becomes anxious, tense, or otherwise difficult; it is like a fine oil that makes the gears of relationship turn smoothly.

Whenever anxiety or fear show up in the form of defensiveness, competitiveness, resistance to negotiating, or tension between you, you can reduce them by following these guidelines:

Exercise: Guidelines for Reassurance

1. Become aware of tension or difficulty:

If your conversation or negotiation begins to feel difficult, your partner is not being cooperative, or you find yourself feeling resistant and uncooperative, that's the time for reassurance.

2. Verify and discuss the emotional atmosphere:

Suggest to your partner that [both] your feelings seem to need some attention, and describe how the emotional climate feels to you. If your partner seems to you to be anxious, use I messages describing what you feel, see, or experience that seems uncomfortable. If you think your partner is tense or anxious, ask for information.

Say: "I need to call a time out. This discussion has begun to feel tense and strained.

How are you feeling? Are you worried about something?" (Or: "I am worried that ...."). Once you have established and understood who is anxious or worried, and why, go on to the next step.

3. Identify and discuss reasons for tension:

Any tension or anxiety between you will either be directly related to what you are discussing (and how you are interacting) or it will be brought in from another source (work stress, an argument with someone else, a bad commute). If things feel anxious, use your active speaking and active listening skills (Chapter Four) to ask what your partner thinks and feels. Ask if you're right about what you're guessing, and if so, ask what it's about and use active listening and attentive speaking to find out if you are being misunderstood, as Rose does:

Rose: (opening discussion) I'm really looking forward to talking with you about the changes I want to make in my life.

John: (arms folded across chest, unsmiling.) What are we supposed to do to work it out?

Rose: (asking for information) John, you look anxious. Are you worried about this?

John: (admits he's anxious) Yes, I don't see how these changes will do anything but create problems.

Rose: (active listening) Are you afraid your life will change in ways you don't like?

John: (confirming) Yes.

4. Offer or ask for reassurance:

Once you identify the source of the tension and/or anxiety, you can make a specific reassurance. For example, if you are anxious because you believe your partner is angry with you, you can ask to be reassured either that your partner is not angry, or that the anger can be resolved, and what you need to do to resolve it. Use your communication skills to determine what reassurance to use. Sometimes the reassurance is spontaneous, as with Rose's response to John's fears:

John: (realizing what he's tense about) Maybe I'm afraid of losing you.

Rose: (spontaneous, warm) Oh, my dear, you couldn't lose me if you tried. I'll be with you for the rest of my life.

John: (relieved, sighs) Phew. That helps a lot. I thought you were getting more independent so you could eventually leave.

Rose: (more considered reassurance) I promise, John, if I ever want to leave, I'll tell you straight out, and not indirectly. OK?

John: (much more relaxed posture) OK. Now, I feel better about talking about this.

5. Continue until the atmosphere becomes more relaxed:

Depending on how long-standing or intense the tension between you is, the above four steps can take a few minutes or much longer. Continue discussing the anxiety, the reasons behind it, and the kind of reassurance that is needed until you feel the tension between you relax. You'll be able to tell this because the signs that indicated tension will change. For example, if you felt a knot in your stomach, your stomach will now feel relaxed.

Or, if you felt the conversation was difficult and halting, it will now flow more smoothly. An atmosphere of heavy seriousness may lighten into laughter. When your original indicators of tension are relaxed, you are ready to resume problem solving. Rose knew John was reassured when he let out a sigh of relief, and then his body relaxed.

If you are unable to reassure each other, or repeated attempts at reassurance don't seem to help, suppressed hurt and anger from past conflicts may be coming to the surface. Try the following exercise for Setting Aside Held Anger and Hurt, and come back to this step again later.

Barrier: Unresolved Anger and Hurt Solution: Set aside held anger and hurt.

Often, when problems are not solved right away, you can store up frustration and disappointment until you feel so angry and hurt we cannot negotiate calmly and rationally. Learning to set aside accumulated feelings will stop them from interfering with your communication and cooperation.

If you have had unsolved problems for a while, either of you may have a backlog of suppressed anger, frustration or hurt feelings: maybe because you felt that expressing them would cause trouble or would accomplish nothing. These stored-up feelings can get in the way because they create emotional and mental turmoil that can interfere with clear thinking. Occasionally, held anger and hurt from some other incident (last week's fight about an unrelated issue) can also interfere if it gets in the way of your good will for one another and of your clear thinking.

Although your unresolved anger and hurt can emerge at any step in the negotiation, it will most often be revealed as you set the stage; you have trouble establishing good will, and reassurance doesn't seem to help.

You can't have a rational discussion until held anger and hurt are resolved, because the emotional turmoil creates an atmosphere which interferes with your thinking, and influences you to see each other as an enemy.

Hurt feelings and anger arise in the course of every long-term relationship. Learning to set aside these intense feelings will benefit you and your partner in many situations in addition to your negotiations, including at work, when problems arise with your children, or when emergencies must be handled in spite of intense feelings.

If Rose has been struggling with her discontent for some time and has had trouble getting John to take her seriously, she could have several months or even a year or two of hurt and resentment stored up about it.

John: Well, here's our negotiation date. (establishing good will) I love you Rose and I sure want to do what I can to make your life together the best it can be for both of us.

Rose: (bitterly) Yeah, as long as it doesn't upset your tidy little nest.

John: (startled, reacting) If you can't be civil, then I don't need this hassle.

Rose: (angry) That's just your style. If it doesn't suit you, you refuse to deal!

(end of discussion)

On the other hand, if Rose and John know how to set aside held anger and hurt, the evening can take quite another turn:

--a little later--

Rose: (thoughtful) John, I'm sorry I blew up a while ago. I took time to write and think about it, and I realized that I've been blaming you for my discontent and resenting that you wouldn't help me work out my problem. I'm not so angry now. In fact, I appreciate your trying to open the negotiation tonight, when it's my problem.

John: (cautious) I didn't realize you were so upset. Maybe we can try it again, but I think we both need a little more time to settle down and cool off. Can we take fifteen minutes, and then come back to it?

Rose: (agreeing) I think that's a good idea. Let's have dessert and coffee, and then try again.

Rose's held anger had been building for a while, and after it erupted, she took a break and wrote in her journal and thought about it. Once she had worked through her held anger, she was able to come back and explain herself to John, and ask to resume the negotiation. John had been caught by surprise, and his anger wasn't held very long, so after requesting a short additional break, he's ready to go again.

How to Set Aside Held Anger and Hurt

A. Discharging

If you or your partner are holding anger or hurt feelings; a period of emotional discharge may be necessary before you can proceed in your negotiation. This may be as simple as saying, "Wait a minute. I'm still angry about this, and I have to refocus on what we're doing." or, if your anger and frustration has been long-standing, it may require taking a break in the negotiation at this point to calm down.

Discharging away from the person you're upset with allows you to express your feelings in a way that doesn't aggravate the problem.

Once your feelings are dealt with, you will be calm and able think clearly enough to return to your partner and solve the problem. You and your partner can learn how to take time out to release and resolve anger, frustration and hurt feelings in a variety of ways:

- Putting it aside temporarily by changing focus,
- Releasing your anger and hurt through physical activity,
- Releasing your feelings by expressing them through writing or talking.
- Releasing by talking with a friend or therapist who will listen.

Depending on the intensity of your held hurt and anger, how longstanding it is, and how comfortable you are with handling your feelings you can choose to discharge by yourself or with the help of another. Whichever you choose, remember, the partner at whom you are angry in the first place will probably not be able to listen objectively enough to help you discharge it.

B. Discharging by yourself

Lower levels of held anger or hurt can be discharged alone, by writing down your feelings, talking out loud to yourself, and simply acknowledging how you feel as in the directions below. Many people think that they have to talk their feelings out with someone else, and this is fine if you happen to have an appropriate friend handy when you need them, or are in therapy. Learning to discharge by yourself keeps you from being overly dependent on others, and is usually much simpler and quicker. The advantages to releasing your help anger and hurt alone are:

1. You can do it when and where you want instead of waiting for the right friend or therapist to be available.
2. It is simpler than making arrangements with another person.

3. It may be easier to be more honest about your hurt and anger to yourself than to another.

4. You can choose a method that suits your personality and the nature of your problem.

5. It doesn't postpone your negotiation as much as making arrangements to talk to someone else does.

We recommend trying to discharge by yourself first, using the guidelines below, and if you find that your held anger and hurt are too intense for you to handle alone; get the help of a friend or therapist.

A. Discharging with a friend

Some people find it easier to release feelings by talking to someone, because they feel heard, cared about and validated and they have someone's implicit permission to discharge. Also, since your friend is uninvolved in the problem, you know that your anger or hurt won't place pressure on or upset him or her.

Very few good friends are objective enough to be good listeners, so when you choose someone, make sure they can hear you without judgement. The listener's role is to be nonjudgmental, dispassionate and supportive. Also, you must be very careful which friend you choose to share your feelings with because if you're talking about your anger and hurt toward your partner, you need a friend who can understand that the feelings are temporary, and listen to you without placing blame, and then forget what you said, so it won't be brought up later.

If attempting to discharge on your own doesn't help, call a friend, read the above description of a good listener, and see if he or she will agree to help you. Then follow the instructions in the guidelines below.

B. Discharging with professional help

In cases where emotions have been pent-up for a long time, involve repeated negative patterns (such as being abandoned, financially devastated or cheated on) from past relationships, or rape, violence, child abuse, or other traumatic history is involved, discharging held hurt and anger is critically important, needs knowledgeable supervision, and can take some time to complete. In these cases, getting into group or individual therapy is essential. If this describes you, and you are not in therapy, get a referral from a friend, a doctor or a local hotline. Your therapist will help you follow the guidelines below or similar methods of discharging.

Guidelines for Setting Aside Held Hurt and Anger

1. Separate from the problem:

In order to discharge effectively, explain that you have feelings that are in the way and request a temporary time-out from problem solving. Say you're too angry, hurt or tense to continue right now and you want a break to take care of your feelings first. Set a new appointment to resume the discussion later, even another day if necessary to reassure your partner that you are not trying to avoid negotiating permanently.

2. Choose a method:

There are three methods of setting aside held anger and hurt, as outlined in the exercises that follow. To choose the appropriate exercise for you, use the following guidelines, which include simple exercises:

Option A: Temporarily Setting Feelings Aside

This is the simplest of the options. John, for example, was able to take a few minutes, let his surprise and hurt subside and simply focus on the negotiation again, because his hurt wasn't long standing or deep but was a result of his conflict and misunderstanding with Rose earlier that same evening.

If it is relatively easy, postpone dealing with your feelings and stay focused on problem solving, with just a short (five to fifteen minute) break. This is the best option to choose for a small upset.

1. Focus on your feelings to figure out what they are.

2. See if you can set it aside for now and continue the negotiation.

3. If you decide to postpone expressing it, focus on your desire to resolve the problem you are negotiating and your respect and love for your partner. Allow the anger or hurt to fade into the background as you move your attention to the negotiation.

4. Return to your partner and resume negotiation.

A. Release through physical activity

Emotions that are pent-up can often be released through physical activity. The exercise will loosen the muscles holding the tension and allow you to release some of the held emotion, so you can get back to negotiating. Choose this option if you enjoy physical activity and you often experience a change of mood after exercising.

1. Select almost any exercise, such as a brisk walk, dancing to music with a steady, pulsing beat, shooting baskets, ball, bicycling, jogging, Tai Chi, yoga, swimming, wrestling, punching a pillow or a punching bag, or throwing something repeatedly in a safe setting (a large, pillow or catalog thrown at a soft bed or couch is energetic and safe, as is hitting a bucket of golf balls, or throwing or hitting a ball against a wall as in tennis, handball or racquetball, or beating a mattress with a tennis racquet or a bat) and set aside a time to handle these feelings through that activity.

   When you begin your workout you may feel your held emotion as tension in your body, usually the midsection area, stomach, chest, shoulders, back, neck head or jaws.

2. As you exercise, pay attention to your feelings and whatever tension you feel in your body, and try to continue your workout until the intensity of your hurt and anger are reduced and you can reconnect with the good feelings you have toward your partner, and can focus on the task of problem solving.

3. Return to your partner and resume negotiation.

F: Release with Verbal or Written Expression

Choose this option if you often use writing or talking out loud (to yourself or to a friend) to help you understand how you feel and what you want to do. Held emotions are exactly that: held. When you express them they lose their pent-up energy, and become much easier to resolve.

1. Find a place to be alone and uninterrupted for whatever time you need to write or talk your feelings out. You can express your feelings in whatever way feels best to you: write or draw in your journal, pray or talk out loud. The more you express your feelings, the easier it will be to let them go and get back to solving the problem.

2. Keep expressing your feelings in until you feel a release or relief. You may also discover the central reason for the feelings, often in the form of a new idea. For example, John told himself how angry he was while he took a shower, and after a few minutes, he suddenly realized, "Oh! I'm angry at Rose because she surprised me by being angry when I was ready to negotiate, and feeling my caring for her. I felt ambushed. When she apologized, I wasn't ready to forgive her yet. I think I'm ready now, because it doesn't seem so important anymore." When you feel your tension release, you'll find that it's easier to think clearly, and you can go on with problem-solving

3. Return to your partner and resume negotiation.

4. Mastering these skills and steps of setting the stage, including: set time and place, establish good will, reassure, and set aside held anger and hurt will enable you to create an inviting atmosphere in which it will be easy to think clearly and solve the problem.

Once you have completed the steps to setting the stage, you are ready to move on to the final phases of cooperative negotiation. In the next chapter, you will learn about stating and exploring wants, a key step of the Negotiating Tree which stimulates and releases your creativity. With it, you will discover new solutions that can satisfy both of you. Creativity makes this step of cooperative problem solving fun because it allows you to free up your imagination and brainstorm successfully.

Chapter Five

State and Explore Your Wants

Once you have set the stage, you and your partner can focus on solving the problem, as a team, without being distracted by old anger and hurt or by interruptions. Stating and exploring wants is the first step of the Negotiation Tree where you both begin to contribute to the problem solving process, and participate equally in stating what you want. To be able to work together to get both your wants satisfied, you must first state clearly what you want; and to communicate what you want, you must first know what you want.

We have found that many couples have difficulty solving problems because they do not know what they want, or, if they do know, cannot express it to a partner. If that's a problem for either or both you, here's what you need to learn to build a lasting, sustainable relationship. Many of us are taught, from early childhood on, that our wants are selfish and that we should be polite and let others wants come first ("Be polite, let Susie have the toy"). We are made to feel that it isn't OK to want ("Don't even ask me for a cookie just before dinner"), or, that we can't have what we want ("Of course you can't have a new toy, do you think I'm made of money?") or that, if we get what we want, someone else will be deprived (a belief in scarcity).

In response, some of us learn (perhaps in competition with brothers and sisters or schoolmates) to grab what we can get, without considering whether we want it or not.

These internalized demands, prohibitions and restrictions make us anxious about getting what we want and even convinced that we won't, which in turn leads us to compete, to rescue, and not to know and state what we want, so we can come up with creative and effective ways to get it. In addition to all these other restrictions on wanting, you may have the idea that the consequences of wanting are bad (no one will like you), and so it is too scary to know what you want. Because knowing what you want sometimes means you risk being disappointed (there may be a real reason why you can't get it), and many people have an exaggerated idea of how bad disappointment feels (if I don't get what I want I'll be miserable), they avoid wanting at all (thus unconsciously guaranteeing that they won't be able to get it, because you can't negotiate for a want you don't know about).

When you let each other know what you want in a helpful, non-threatening way, you help each other know what it will take to satisfy each of you. If you don't know what your partner wants, you can wind up with a false or one-sided solution that will leave one or both of you feeling unsatisfied, overpowered, or manipulated. When you state what you want, it's like putting all the true facts on the table, just as you lay all the pieces of a jigsaw puzzle out, so you can see them better, and more easily solve your puzzle.

There is a big difference between expressing what you want and making a demand. Stating what you want is an effort to communicate clearly, so you and your partner can both be satisfied, while demanding is selfishly insisting that your get what you want, without regard for each other's wants and feelings. Selfishness and greed are driven by a belief in scarcity and fear of not getting enough. Saying what you want leads to successful problem solving and cooperation. If you believe that saying what you want is the same as insisting on having it, you might suppress your awareness of what you want, which makes it difficult, if not impossible, to solve a problem.

Your natural awareness of what you want is probably suppressed if:

- You go blank when you try to think of what you want.

- You believe you don't care what the result is, but you feel unhappy or resentful later.
- You feel dissatisfied, but you can't put your Feeling into words, or think what to do about it.
- You get anxious, depressed or angry when a problem needs to be solved, because you feel you'll lose.
- You want what everyone else wants, what you think you should want, or what someone else has, but you can't think of what you want on your own.

In the last chapter, John and Rose had set the stage for their negotiation, and now it's after supper, and they're settling down to talk, but neither of them has taken the time to think about what they want:

John: (taking responsibility and cooperating in the negotiation) Ok, Rose, you said you had a problem now that the kids were grown, and you felt unneeded. What do you think would fix it?

Rose: (vague) Oh, I don't know. Maybe we could do more together.

John: (defensive) Rose, you know that's not possible. I'm too busy at work. Be realistic.

Rose: (feeling helpless and confused) I'm just so depressed. I don't know what to do.

John: (taking over) You need to go see a doctor, like I said before.

Rose: (giving up) Oh, I guess you're right. (End of discussion)

Because Rose doesn't clearly know what she wants, both she and John are too confused and vague to reach a solution, so they end up discouraged and frustrated.

Barriers to Stating Wants

When you first try to say what you want, your anxiety about the differences in your wants can tempt you to fall back into the old habit of rescuing your partner and not stating your wants fully and clearly. Or, by not listening to each other, you may create a power struggle.

Arguing (either verbally or silently) with what your partner wants makes it impossible to hear and understand your partner's position.

Fear that you can't both have what you want may cause either of you to:

- Exaggerate what you want: (power struggle)

If you say you want more than you really do, ("I want you here all the time") you'll confuse yourself and your partner, and make the problem look harder than it is.

- Overstate your need: (power struggle)

The fear that you won't get what you want may cause you to state it as if your survival depended on it ("I'll just die if you don't come with me.") This feels like coercion and manipulation, and your partner will resist cooperating with you.

- Argue for or justify what you want: (power struggle)

If you believe what you want is not important or won't be honored, you may present them as a persuasive argument, with an overwhelming flood of reasons why you should want them or they should be satisfied, ("I should get more of the money than you do, because ...") which can provoke your partner to object and argue in return, rather than listen.

- Not say what you want: (rescue)

Belief that differences in what you and your partner want will cause a fight may lead you to say you "don't care" or "it's not important" or just be silent, when the truth is you'll resent not getting what you want.

- Understate what you want: (rescue)

Fear that your partner will be upset, hurt or unhappy may lead you to ask for something else ("I want to go to a movie" when you really want an evening all alone together) which confuses your partner, and makes it impossible to solve the problem. By not clearly stating what you want, you make it impossible for your partner to clearly understand your position, and, as Don and Dale discover, create competition and struggle rather than cooperation and a mutually satisfying solution.

Don and Dale have defined the problem that both of them want the back bedroom for an office, and set the stage for their negotiation, but when they try to solve the problem, they run into trouble:

Don: (stating want, justifying) I want to use the back bedroom for my office. I'm spending too much on office space.

Dale: (stating want, beginning to justify) I want to use the back bedroom for my office, too, because from there I can keep an eye on Kendra as she plays in the back yard.

Don: (gets competitive) I could always keep an eye on her, and you could use the dining room. Besides, you only work part time, and I work full time, so I deserve it more.

Dale: (getting angry, arguing) The dining room is dark and everyone tramps through it all the time coming in and out and I think it's about time I had a decent place to work. Besides, if you ran your business better, you'd easily be able to afford the rent on the office you already have.

Don and Dale find themselves in an argument, and no longer negotiating about what they want, because they aren't listening to each other; and they're both locked in competing, trying to win, because they have reverted to believing that only one of them will get what he wants. When they use better communication techniques, such as I messages and active listening, remember to focus on stating their own wants, listen more carefully to each other, and support each other in stating their wants, the discussion has a better outcome:

Don: (stating want) I want to use the back bedroom for my office. My business isn't doing as well as it was, and I need to cut my expenses.

Dale: (active listening) Well, I understand that you want that room for an office. It would be cheaper for you. (stating want) I want it too. I want to be where it's quiet and has more light, and also where I can watch Kendra play in the yard.

Don: (active listening) You want more light, less traffic and noise, and to be able to see Kendra in the yard?

Dale: (confirms) Right. It sounds like our wants are clear. Is there anything you'd like to add?

Don: Only that it also sounds great to work here, from home.

Dale: It sounds good to me, too.

Don: (ready for the next step) OK, shall we explore our options? Let's put our heads together and see if there's a way we can both get what we want.

Dale: Yes. I think we can do it.

Don and Dale's first attempt became competitive, because they were each afraid to lose, and they began arguing with each other about why one of them deserved the office more. In the second attempt, they began to cooperate, acting on the assumption that they could find a mutually satisfactory solution, and seeking to work together.

Using active listening and I messages, they were able to stay focused on stating their wants and hearing each other, without jumping to conclusions or arguing, and therefore keep their focus on solving the problem to their mutual satisfaction.

Exercise: Overcoming the Barriers to Wanting

This exercise will show you how to break down the barriers that stop you from knowing what you want; and to help you understand what you want that may have been suppressed since childhood. This series of seven steps will help you discover the ways you stifle your wants and develop alternatives so that you can easily know and communicate what you want when you are problem solving.

If you have a lot of trouble with wanting you may wish to repeat it several times, over a period of days or weeks, until you become completely comfortable with identifying and accepting your wants.

1. Discovering your childhood wants:

Read this exercise slowly, pausing where you see three dots in a row, to allow time for the fantasy to form. You may find it easier to record the instructions and play them back to give freedom to your imagination.

Do not stifle what you want by criticizing or questioning them or insisting that they be logical or make sense, but allow them to come out as they are; impossible or fantastic wishes are OK.

Close your eyes, and picture yourself as a young child, about 7 years old... alone in a favorite place from your childhood.... You might see your child self in your room... or outdoors in a special hiding place... where you used to go... Now pretend a wizard (or a magician, a genie, or a fairy godmother) comes to you... and says you can have any wishes you can name in 5 minutes... Allow your seven-year-old self to imagine anything at all... what do you imagine? What do you wish for...? Wish for all the material things you want ...toys, ice cream, new Reeboks, jewels, money... wish for love and happiness, praise and encouragement... wish for friends your own age, and grownup people who care about you... whatever you want.

Now, slowly open your eyes, review what just happened in your fantasy, and write down your wants. Head the page My Childhood Want list.

Here's how Joe's childhood want list looked:

My childhood want list

A sailboat

cowboy boots

plenty of time to play

never have to go to the dentist

lots of money

fly a plane

be a baseball pro

be Superman

have a Batmobile

lots of hugs and snuggles

a secret friend to have a clubhouse with

This list has some possible and impossible ideas on it, all quite natural for the seven year old Joe, which shows that he's in touch with his natural, childlike ability to want, and able to be creative without judging and stifling what he wants. If your list sounds childlike, you are getting in touch with your natural ability to want; if your wants sound too adult, ("I want more stability in my life", "A better job") repeat the exercise and spend more time on establishing your picture of a seven-year-old you. When you feel that your list is complete, move on to Step 2.

2. Discovering your wants today:

Do not criticize or question what you want, just allow it to come out as naturally as possible. Imagine anything at all, no matter how impossible, illogical or fantastic it sounds. If an item comes up expressed in terms of "I don't want...." that's OK, too.

Now, imagine as you did before, but this time see yourself as the grownup you are today:

Close your eyes, and picture yourself as you are now... alone in that same favorite place from your childhood.... a special hiding place... where you used to go... Now pretend a wizard (or a magician, a genie, or a fairy godmother) comes to you ...and says you can have any wishes you can name in 5 minutes...what do you wish for...? Wish for all the material things you want ... a sports car, a boat, a mink, win the lottery, be very famous.... and also the nonmaterial: love and happiness, success, praise and encouragement... wish for friends, people who care about you, good sex...

Now, slowly open your eyes, review what just happened in your fantasy, head your list My Wants Today and write down your wishes.

Here's Joe's grownup list:

My Wants Today

- $6,000/mo. net
- A sailboat
- Not to work.
- Not to feel stressed.
- Not to worry about money.
- No relationship hassles.
- Cowboy boots

- A thriving business consulting and teaching
- Six months off
- '55 Chevy: cherry condition
- Uninhibited sex with Michelle
- New computer with graphics
- Travel: Jamaica, African safari
- Live in small town
- Season tickets to football
- Mountain bike
- Fly my own Lear jet

Like Joe's grownup list, yours will probably be different from your child list, but contain some related things. Some of the items on your list, as on Joe's, may not seem possible (a Lear jet, for example), but it belongs on the list because it is a want.

3. List and examine what you want:

Review and contemplate both your childhood and your adult want list. As you do this, reasons why you can't have some of your wants will probably come up, or thoughts that the wishes are silly, childish, greedy, not-nice, selfish or wrong. You may think "we can't afford it" or "you don't deserve that; you haven't been good." These internal reasons not to want are what you need to discover and counteract to free up your ability to know what you want. Write down all the reasons you think you can't have what you want in a column opposite your wants, and try not to censor or argue with these negative thoughts, to bring them into your awareness and find out what they are.

When Joe looked at his lists, his internal restrictions and objections sounded like this:

WHAT DO I WANT?	*WHAT'S IN THE WAY?*
$6,000/mo net	I can't earn that much
A sailboat	Can't afford it
Cowboy boots	Won't use them enough
A thriving business consulting and teaching	Can't do a business by myself
Six months off	Can't afford it
'55 Chevy: cherry condition	Too much money
Uninhibited sex with Michelle	She'll never change; sex dies out in long-term relationships
New computer w/better graphics	silly kid stuff
Travel: Jamaica, African safari	too much money, no time
Play professional baseball	too old, not enough skill
Live in small town	can't earn a living
Season tickets to football	too expensive
Mountain bike	I'll probably get hurt

1. Evaluate your objections:

After your list is created, evaluate how realistic your restrictions and objections are. When Joe wrote his restrictions they seemed true, because he has believed them for a long time, but as he reviewed them objectively and thought about them, he realized he felt differently about them; some were obviously false ("I don't deserve it"), some were probably not true ("I'll probably get hurt"), some were actually true ("too old, not enough skill to play pro ball") and some were temporarily true ("I can't afford it"). Go through your own list again, and mark whether the objections are

(F) false,

(PF) probably false,

(TT) temporarily true, or

(T) true.

Now, in order to begin to eliminate some of your inner restrictions and open yourself to what you really want:

When an objection is false (F), cross it out, and let the want stand without an objection.

- When an objection is probably false (PF), make a note about what you need to do to make sure it's not true (Joe wrote: get information about climbing safety, join a climbing club).
- When one is temporarily true, (TT) make some notes about what you'd have to do to make it false, (Joe wrote: get more education, get a better job, win the lottery).
- When you find one that is true, see if you can alter the want or circumstance a bit until your objections become false. (Joe can't be a pro ballplayer, but he can join a local league)

Joe's in the way list reveals some wants that actually are impossible. Playing professional baseball is not possible, at Joe's age, [Joe's objection gets a (T)] and Joe never had professional-level skill. But, adjusting the want a little bit and joining a baseball or softball league in his age group is still very possible, and might provide him with lots of satisfaction.

Other things that he has on the list, like owning a sailboat, may not be possible immediately, (TT) but, if he wants to put in the effort, he could buy a used one and fix it up, or get some friends to share the cost of a sailboat. After research, Joe finds that football season tickets are not too expensive, and crosses that objection out.

In this way, Joe is able to remove some of his reasons for not wanting and open up some possibilities on his want list.

1. What's Scary About Wanting?

When you begin to explore what you want, you may feel vaguely afraid, as if it's greedy, bad, hopeless or wrong to want things; that bad things will happen to you, or you'll be terribly disappointed if you want them too strongly. These are not objections to individual things that you want, but objections to wanting itself.

Write down your own ideas and fantasies about what you think are the bad things that might happen if you want too much. Keep writing things down until you feel you have captured the scariest possible ideas on your paper.

Here's Joe's list as an example:

What am I afraid will happen if I want too much?

- If I get all the things I want there will probably be a catch.
- I'll want things I can't have and be disappointed and dissatisfied.
- To have all that stuff, I'd have to be rich, and to get rich, I'd have to do things that are not nice (con people, exploit customers or employees, cheat on taxes, rob a bank)
- People who get everything they want mostly steal from others, and don't care about others. They are not liked, and they die rich and lonely.
- God will punish me if I get too greedy.
- Something bad will happen.

With fears like these, Joe might have a difficult time allowing himself to know what he wants. However, once these fears, which are left over from childhood, are brought into awareness, they can be resolved, counteracted and reassured, so Joe and you are free to know what you want, and therefore know how to solve your problem.

2. Counteracting Your Fear:

Look at your list of reasons you can't have what you want. Imagine that you are encouraging and supporting a very dear friend of yours. If your friend gave you reasons (like Joe's or yours) why he or she couldn't have what he wanted and be happy, would you accept them without question and advise him or her to give up hope? Chances are you would tell your friend that it is perfectly possible to have everything on the list and be happy, honest and well loved, too. You would explain why you thought his reasons for not getting what he wants were wrong, and reassure his fears by suggesting solutions for them which are encouraging, and stimulate his hope, creativity and clearer thinking.

By doing two things, you can learn to reassure yourself when your objections to wanting get in the way:

1. For each fear on your list, find a solution. That is, consider what you might do to

- solve the fearful outcome if it happens,
- avoid it happening in the first place,
- to be more creative about finding a non-fearful way of getting what you want, or
- reassure or rebut your dire prediction.

2. Write these solutions next to your fears.

Here's how Joe counteracted his scary list:

FEARS ABOUT WANTING

I'll want all the things I can't have and be disappointed and dissatisfied. I'll be miserable.

To have all that stuff, I'd have to be rich, and to get rich, I'd have to do things that are not nice (con people, exploit customers or employees, cheat on taxes, rob a bank)

HOW TO TAKE THE FEAR OUT

I can look more closely at my wants to see which ones I want enough to actually get. I can divide them into easy, medium and difficult categories, and I can meet as many of my wants as I can, enjoy those, and not let the others spoil my fun.

I can be rich, honest and fair, too. There are honest ways to make money and my wealth could benefit the community. Also, I can be happy whether or not I'm rich.

FEARS ABOUT WANTING

People who get everything they want mostly steal from others, and don't care about others. They are not liked, and they die rich and lonely.

HOW TO TAKE THE FEAR OUT

Not true. Many of the best things in life can't be bought with money. People also get legitimately successful in business, inherit, win lotteries, and are loved.

Rose and John realize from their earlier unsuccessful attempt that they need to get clear about what they want, so they do this exercise.

The resulting summary of Rose's and John's wants might look like this:

ROSE

I want something meaningful to do.

I want more time for me.

I want to preserve our marriage

I want you to be happy, too.

JOHN

I want you to be a support system for me, run errands, prepare meals, and entertain business associates.

I want you to be available, like you always have.

I want to preserve our marriage.

I want you to be happy, too.

Now that their wants are clearly expressed, Rose and John can understand each other. The problem is clear, which will make it easier to find solutions, and the discussion goes differently:

John: (taking responsibility and cooperating in the negotiation) Ok, Rose, you said you had a problem now that the kids were grown, and you felt unneeded. What do you think would fix it?

Rose: (clearly stating what she wants) Well, John, I've been thinking about it, and I know I want to find something meaningful to do. I'm a caretaker by nature, and I'm sure someone can use my skills. At the same time, I don't want to disrupt our relationship, or make you unhappy. I know you're used to having me here. So, I need to find out what's most important to you about the way we've always done things.

John: (stating his wants) I know that you're unhappy, and I would much prefer to see you happy. But I still need you as my support system, and I don't want to lose that. I want to be able to call you up and ask you to do something for me, or bring home business associates for dinner, or just have my usual dinner at the usual time. It really lessens my job stress to have your support.

Rose: (considering possibilities) That doesn't sound too difficult. If I volunteered or took some classes, I might not always be able to be there at the very moment you want me, but I was often gone when the kids had to go to the doctor or something, and we always worked that out. Maybe we could work this out, too.

As Rose and John are now finding, when they remain calm and centered, and clearly state their wants, the problem will then easily be solved. The energy they would have previously lost to arguing can be put into carrying out the solution to the problem.

Once you have counteracted each fear, you can replace it with encouragement, as in Step Seven.

1. What's good about what I want:

You can encourage yourself to know what you want. For each item in your solutions list, make a statement that uses it as the solution to your fears about wanting.

Joe's solutions looked like this:

In order to get what I want, I must first know what I want.

If I had lots of money, I could help my friends and others who are needy.

Wanting not to take advantage of people makes me proud.

Whether I'm rich or not, I don't want to hurt anyone.

I can have love in my life whether or not I have money.

I know people who know what they want, go for it, and are happy.

Even if what I want seems impossible now, I can probably do it step by step.

You can use these positive statements to encourage yourself, show them to your partner to use as encouragement for you (and, conversely, use your partner's positive statements when he or she needs encouragement) whenever you have difficulty giving yourself permission to want what you want.

If your list has several items that you don't want, you can turn them around;

2. Getting from don't want to want:

The opposite of anything you don't want can turn out to be what you do want. Review your Wants Today list, in Step 2, and pick out anything you listed as something you don't want, or, if you are presently negotiating, and can only think of what you don't want, use that.

Joe's Don't wants were:

 not to work.

not to feel stressed.

not to worry about money. no relationship hassles.

Now, take your don't want list, and opposite each item, list the want that's implied in the don't want. For example, "I don't want to hurt any more" becomes "I want to feel happy and secure".

Here's Joe's turned around list:

- not to work BECOMES have plenty of money. not to feel stressed. BECOMES learn to chill.
- not to worry about money BECOMES have more money, learn how to manage it better, or just lighten up about it
- no relationship hassles BECOMES Learn to solve problems with Michelle better, have more fun

Once you know how to turn a don't want into a want, you can do this anytime you or your partner are trying to solve a problem, but feel stumped about what you want.

Even now that you know what you want; it isn't always easy to communicate your wants clearly to your partner. You may have difficulty expressing what you want, because you are worried about your partner's reaction to it, or hearing and understanding your partner's wants because you're too concerned about what you want. To solve the problem cooperatively, however, each of you needs to know what the other one wants.

Guidelines for Sharing Wants

Any time you and your partner are having trouble communicating, the following five steps will help you effectively take the extra time you need to make sure your wants are clear to each other, so you can understand exactly what will solve the problem and then, by continuing to follow The Negotiation Tree, you can find a mutually satisfactory solution.

1. Set the stage (Chapter Five)

If the atmosphere of mutual cooperation you originally created by Setting the Stage has deteriorated, and you are feeling frustrated, competitive or discouraged, recreate a positive atmosphere by repeating that step. Make sure you have plenty of time and a private place, establish your good feelings about your relationship and each other, and set aside hurt and anger for the purpose of the discussion. This will make it much easier to think clearly, communicate well, and hear each other, because you will begin by being calm and reassured.

2. Use your communication skills (Chapter Four):

One partner speaks first, expressing your wants in the form of I messages. Using attentive speaking to be sure your wants are being heard will make expressing your wants much more effective and efficient. Each of you will try to hear all these wants, using active listening to reassure each other that you're both being heard.

3. Reassure each other (Chapter Four):

When you or your partner shows signs of needing reassurance (gets silent, withdraws, argues) do these three things:

1. use active listening and attentive speaking to find out your partner's fears,

2. reassure your partner with positive messages from Guidelines for Reassurance (Chapter 4) or

3. with direct answers about what you'll do if the worst happens, as in the Guidelines to calm the situation down and get back to sharing your wants.

4. Remember you are sharing wants not resolving conflict:

Here, your only task is to understand what your partner wants, and communicate what you want.

Questioning whether what your partner wants is OK, arguing with or criticizing what your partner wants or suggesting solutions is premature and will create defensiveness and competitiveness between you. Working out any differences you have comes in a later step in The Negotiation Tree.

5. Say exactly what you want, not more, not less:

Monitor what you say to be sure you are not using any of the barriers to wanting (exaggerating, understating, overstating, justifying or arguing, or not saying your wants) to avoid or manipulate your partner's response. If you find that you're using any of these manipulations, or you get confused about what you want, go back to the Problem Solver Inventory and review them, then come back to your partner and restate them as clearly and calmly as you can.

As you become more adept at stating and exploring wants, you'll find that because you care about each other's wants, it is easier to maintain an attitude of cooperation and avoid struggling or competing. Knowing what you want, being able to communicate that clearly with your partner, and turning don't wants into wants helps each of you to be better understood, and makes it easier for both of you to work together to get both your wants met. This frees you to move on to the final steps of The Negotiation Tree, exploring options and deciding, which will show you how to fulfill both your own and your partner's wants.

Chapter Six

Explore Your Options and Decide

Now that you and your partner know how to identify and communicate what you want, you are about to discover one of three things:

1. You want nearly the same thing:

What each of you wants is so similar or compatible that the solution is obvious, and the problem is solved. It was merely your lack of understanding, miscommunication, or lack of awareness of what both of you wanted that made it look like there was a problem. When that happens, it's not necessary to explore options because the problem is already solved for you, like John and Rose's problem in the last chapter. If clarifying your wants has led you to believe that your problem is virtually solved, you can skip directly to the section called Deciding and Confirming Your Decision later in this chapter.

2. You're closer to a solution than you think:

What you both want seems compatible, but you haven't come to a definite solution. In this case, you will feel reassured by knowing what you both want, and proceed to creatively explore new options (Brainstorm) and discuss them until the solution becomes clear.

When Carol and Joe clarified their wants about housework, they found that both of them wanted someone else to do it, which left them with clear, compatible wants, but no solution as yet.

3. You still disagree:

Your different wants still seem in conflict or appear to be unsolvable. Often, although your wants are clear, and you both understand them, if there is a conflict in the wants you have expressed, a mutually satisfactory solution isn't obvious:

- Paul might want a beach vacation (to swim and relax in the sun) while Mary wants to go to the mountains (to hike and get exercise and clean air).
- Fred might want sex three times a week, and Naomi might prefer once every two weeks.
- Don and Dale might struggle over what seems like not enough space in the house for both of them to have their offices there.

When your wants seem to be in such conflict, finding a mutually satisfactory solution is more difficult than when they are compatible, but not at all impossible. Here you can learn to find a workable, mutually satisfying solution without competition, power plays or rescues.

Exploring your options is the problem solving part of solving a problem: developing possible solutions (options), determining the best ones and making a decision.

You have already done all the work to create an atmosphere of cooperation, establish mutual caring and communicate clearly; so this is the easiest step of negotiating. Here you both get to play with ideas, to consider both fantastic and practical options, and to pool your creative energy by brainstorming. When you approach the problem creatively, you can to develop ideas and options you would not have thought of when you were arguing. New options will break your stalemate and help you find a mutually satisfactory solution.

When brainstorming isn't enough, you be able to experiment and explore new possibilities. Whether your problem is simple, like who does what around the house, or complex, such as solving sexual problems or working out money worries, following the guidelines and techniques in this chapter will lead you to success.

Skills and Barriers in Exploring Options

When you have many possible solutions to choose from, you can find mutually satisfactory solution.

The skills you will learn to facilitate solving problems:

- brainstorming
- How to creatively think of new options until you have enough to solve the problem
- the abundance worksheet
- A tool to teach you how to gain a deeper understanding of the dynamics underlying the problem, and look at it from a new, more creative perspective
- research and experimenting
- A way to gather more information when you can't figure out a mutually satisfactory solution
- deciding
- A simple process of picking the best option out of several
- confirming the decision
- To make sure you have not overlooked any confusion or misunderstanding in your choice
- celebration,
- How to acknowledge and confirm your successful decision, and create confidence in your ability to solve problems and enthusiasm for the next negotiation, and
- renegotiation, which will take the pressure off your decision making and help you accommodate unexpected life changes.

The barriers that are likely to get in the way of solving problems are:

- apparent scarcity:

    When you feel anxious that the problem is unsolvable, you can be tempted to compete or give up, which will prevent you from finding the cooperative solution.

164

- hopelessness:

  When you try to solve all possible aspects: (like the unfixable past, and the unforeseeable future) of the problem now, you'll both be discouraged and creative thinking will be difficult.

- confusion:

  Reaching an unclear agreement; which leads to thinking you have the problem solved when you don't.

- criticism:

  When you are critical of suggested ideas, your creativity is stifled, and it is harder to suggest new options, which limits the possible solutions to the problem.

Brainstorming

If the solution isn't clear after you share what you want with each other, you need to come up with new ideas until you find a satisfactory one. It can be difficult to develop new options id you don't break the habitual thinking that blocks creativity:

- Rigid or limited ideas: (shoulds) If you can only do things in certain, preset ways (such as the way your family did it), it will prevent you from considering new options that may suit you better.

- Criticism: Can stifle new ideas by attacking them for not being perfect before they are even fully formed, and

- Ingrained thinking habits: Can prevent you from seeing possible solutions because you have never considered them before.

If you're feeling stuck, you can stir your creative imagination by learning to brainstorm; a technique developed by high-powered think tank scientists and used in high-tech firms like Apple to invent new solutions for previously unsolvable science and technology problems. The object is to develop a list of ideas; many may be useless, but enough will be fresh and feasible to choose from.

Brainstorming was created to overcome limitations on creativity and it will help you and your partner free up your thinking and explore options.

Your creativity is limited when you:

- see a problem only one way,
- are so accustomed to a particular way of doing things that other ideas don't occur to you,
- approach problem solving with a perfectionistic, hopeless, or critical attitude,
- have been taught by your family or society that an option is unthinkable (you shouldn't do it), and
- don't have enough information.

When you brainstorm, you overcome criticism blockage by getting playful and energetic, and accepting even silly or impossible ideas in the process. When you are not worried by whether options are reasonable, you give your creativity free reign. You list as many kinds of ideas as you possibly can. Brainstorming breaks through old familiar concepts and stimulates a free flow new, more creative ideas by being playful, rapid-fire, and excited.

Exercise: Brainstorming

Choose a place where you won't be interrupted, and allow enough time. Write on a whiteboard, chalkboard, large pad or computer screen you both can see. Standing and writing is good because physically moving around helps you to stay loose and energized.

1. Write the problem down.

Write down the problem and each of your basic wants and keep it in plain sight while you brainstorm. Having it in front of you will help you stay on track.

Don and Dale wrote: We both want the back bedroom for an office, and there's not enough room for both of us.

Paul and Mary, negotiating their vacation wants, wrote: How to have a vacation in mountainous pine forest and sun on a beach, too.

For *Carol and Joe*, the statement read: How to take the burden of housework off Carol without putting it on Joe.

2. Write as many ideas as you can in ten minutes:

Each of you write ideas on the board or pad as you come up with them to keep you moving, and raise the energy level. Set a timer for ten minutes. During that time, each of you contribute as many ideas as you can, call them out and write them down. Saying your ideas out loud as well as writing them creates a playful atmosphere, like a game of charades or a TV game show.

Be silly, be boisterous, shout ideas out, don't worry about being sensible or reasonable, get as excited as a gameshow contestant. Remember, the first ideas may be hesitant, but as you get into the game and begin to toss ideas back and forth, your energy will rise. The more your energy flows, the more your ideas will flow. Don't criticize or comment on the ideas. You can evaluate each other's ideas later.

Paul and Mary's session went like this:

Mary: (playful) Cut down a tree and take it to the beach!

    Paul: (joining in) I know: play Russian roulette, and the winner goes to Rio on the life insurance!

    Mary: Separate vacations!

    Paul: We'll split our time in half; one week at the beach, one week in the mountains!

    Mary: Alternate days by helicopter!

    Paul: Double our vacation time this year and do two weeks at each place!

    Mary: (suddenly inspired) Wait! How about a mountain lake?

    Paul: (enthused) Lake Tahoe!

    Mary: (more ideas) Pine Mountain Lake!

While Don and Dale were slightly more serious:

Don: (starting serious, getting lighter) You take the back bedroom, I'll take the master bedroom and we'll sleep in the back yard.

Dale: (thinking) You take space in one of those executive suites with a receptionist.

Don: Put Kendra in day care and you rent an office so I can have the back bedroom.

Dale: (having fun) Let's flip a coin to decide and go to the beach right now.

Don: I take a salaried job instead of working for myself.

Dale: (doesn't mean it) I'll take a salaried job and you work at home and take care of Kendra.

Don: Get real successful at our businesses, so we can have more money and buy a bigger place.

Dale: (wild idea) Rob a bank.

Don: Whoever has the bedroom office takes care of Kendra.

Dale: Use the living room for your office, and I can use the back bedroom.

Don: (inspired) Maybe I could find a low-rent office suite and sublet some of it to cover the rent.

Dale: (enthused) Maybe Tom and Julie would want to share the space rent with you.

Don: Let's keep it the way it is while we research the low rent office suite idea and see if someone wants to sublet from me. If that works, and I get free or low office rent, I'd be happy to let you have the extra bedroom.

3. When your ten minutes are up, review your list.

Enjoy the wild or silly suggestions (such as fly by helicopter or rob a bank). Underline the ones that work for each of you. If there is an option both of you like, proceed to clarify and confirm your decision later in this chapter.

Paul and Mary instantly agreed on a mountain lake, now they only have to decide which one.

When Don and Dale review their suggestions, four of them stand out as feasible

1. Get real successful at our businesses, so we can have more money and buy a bigger place.
2. Find a low-rent office suite and sublet some of it to cover the rent.
3. Find someone to share outside office rent with Don.
4. Keep it the way it is while we research the low rent office suite idea and see if someone wants to sublet from me. If that works, and I get free or low office rent, I'd be happy to let you have the bedroom.

4. Brainstorm again if needed:

If there is no idea that's immediately right for both of you, follow steps 1-3 again. You may need to do several ten-minute brainstorming sessions to loosen up enough to reach a solution that works for both of you. The more fun you have the more creative you'll be; just stay focused on solving the problem. Once you get creative about your solutions, the obvious ones usually show up, as they did with Paul and Mary.

You're searching for solutions that meet both of your wants: Paul and Mary's vacation dilemma was solved by going to a mountain lake which had a beach. Fred and Naomi discovered, after some intimate conversation and creative negotiation, some acceptable and enjoyable (for both partners) ways Fred could seduce Naomi, and also ways Fred could be satisfied with masturbation with cuddling, erotic movies, and one-sided sexual sessions, (where Naomi helped out, but was not equally involved). Don and Dale came up with a number of acceptable ideas, which they will explore below. Carol and Joe resolved their problem by bringing in a cleaning service every two weeks and starting a savings fund for a dishwasher.

Apparent Scarcity

If you are still having trouble stating and exploring wants, the problem may that one or both of you believe there is no possible solution because isn't enough of something (time, money, love, patience, food, good will, space, energy) to go around. That is an apparent scarcity, because the scarcity only appears real. What appears to be a scarcity is usually created by competition, and almost always disappears when carefully examined in terms of what the partners really want.

In Don and Dale's first attempt at discussion, they began by stating wants, but soon became anxious, competitive and got distracted from the problem of how to redistribute house and office space. There was no mutually agreeable solution, because they never tried to find one.

If you fear disappointment or loss, your natural reaction is to defend your share and compete for what you want. You are less able to hear your partner's wants, or to state your own calmly and without exaggeration; which can create the very scarcity you fear, as it did with Don and Dale, whose anxiety prevented them from seeing any options in their first discussion, but who came up with many when tried brainstorming.

Overcoming Apparent Scarcity

The perception of scarcity arises from false limits placed on the problem. Creating abundance depends on expanding these limits. This can be done in two ways:

1. Examine your wants:

It's easy to come up with an instant idea of what you want, without stopping to think about why you want it, or whether it will really satisfy you.

Don said he wanted to use the back bedroom for his office because he wanted to save money and he felt isolated alone in his office. His actual, underlying wants were to save money and have some company, but he passed over them and came up with a possible solution, which he presented to Dale as his want. To Dale it felt like a pre-set decision; which be unfair, so he resisted.

When what you want seems at odds with what your partner wants, take time to examine exactly what you want, why you want it, and if there are any other options. It can help you break through some of the limits, and make it much easier to reach a mutually satisfying solution.

2. Expand your boundaries:

Expanding your boundaries means becoming aware of false ideas or family and cultural taboos that you shouldn't or can't do something that keep you from considering options that would resolve your apparent scarcity:

Don had settled on the back bedroom as the only solution, but when he realized he was limiting his options, he discovered many possibilities (saving to add on the house, sharing a rented office suite, renting a mobile home and parking it in the driveway, making the dining room into his office so Dale could use the back bedroom, or converting part of the garage).

Naomi and Fred's sexual problems cause them to believe there is scarcity in their relationship. Fred is dissatisfied with the frequency and availability of sexual relations with Naomi, and Naomi feels a lack of cuddling and affection. When they explored their options, Fred discovered that paying a little extra affectionate attention (hand holding, hugging, casual touching during the day, sitting close while watching TV) to Naomi got her interested in being sexual with him much more often, and Naomi discovered that when she wasn't feeling as sexual as Fred, he was satisfied with masturbating while she held him, or watching erotic movies together, as long as she was happy, too.

When you are only looking in one place or one moment for the solution to your problem, you'll perceive a lack of options.

For example:

- In workshops, we gave a group of 10 people three or four grapes and told them "There is enough to go around." Nearby, and visible there were several pounds of grapes, but our participants tended to focus on how 10 people might share 4 grapes, never noticing that there was an ample supply close by. Even though we never said they were limited to the grapes we handed them, they automatically limited their boundaries to what they were given. Most of them said they "didn't think to look around" or "thought they shouldn't ask for more grapes" although there were no such rules. You may be limiting your own options in a similar way.

- Although neither Ed nor Carol want to do housework, they don't consider bringing in a cleaning service to do it, so they have an apparent scarcity (of someone who is willing to do it).

- You or your partner may think you have to have a solution right now when you actually have a few days, or weeks, and in that extra time, you can easily find a mutually satisfactory option.

It is easier to think of options for some problems (how to get the car fixed) than for others (a sexual problem, or how to take care of an aged parent.) Whenever a problem seems to be unsolvable; or you feel helpless or hopeless about solving it, you may be facing an apparent scarcity. The abundance worksheet helps you see that there are solutions and you will feel reassured, more hopeful and able to think more clearly.

Even the best of solutions may not be workable forever, because situations and people change, so renegotiation will help you be flexible and able to adapt to change, and make finding a working solution less overwhelming. Being able to renegotiate at any time means you don't have to be able to predict what might happen in the future in order to reach a decision today, because you can renegotiate if the situation changes.

The abundance worksheet is designed to help you break out of this kind of limited thinking, expand your boundaries and discover new options which make problem solving easy. It is a tool for you and your partner to use to get you moving again when you can't find suitable options due to a conflict between your wants.

Don and Dale used the abundance worksheet to find out what lay behind each of their wants for an office, they could understand each other better, feel less afraid of being unsatisfied, and work together to find a mutual solution. We've shown you how they did each step as an example to follow.

Exercise: The Abundance Worksheet

1. Describe the apparent scarcity:

The purpose of this step is to you state your wants, where you disagree, and what the limits seem to be. List both your wants, arguments, explanations and rationalizations of why you want what you want, and the limits you see to run into, all together. Then, pare down your original description until you can develop a summary sentence or two that states what the problem appears to be.

Dale wants back bedroom for office. Don wants it, too. Limited rooms are available. Work at home saves child care expense and is better for child. Eliminate travel time and expense to work, wear on car. Save cost of office rent.

Summary: We both want the back bedroom for an office, and there's not enough room for both of us.

2. Explore wants:

The purpose of this step is to delve more deeply into what you want, and to discover the wants behind your stated wants. It's OK to include what you don't want, because as you have seen in the previous exercise, you can turn your don't wants around and they become wants.

Do this by asking yourself the following questions:

- "Why do I want what I've stated as my wants?" "
- What would having it accomplish, change or solve for me?"
- "What about the current situation makes me dissatisfied or unhappy, and how will getting what I want solve it?"

Once you have answered these questions, you'll be able to write a list of what you want, ending with what your ideal option is, like Don and Dale's:

DON'S WANTS

I want the back bedroom for an office because:

I need to reduce my overhead I hate commuting

I don't like being isolated at my current office.

I want equal rights and equal opportunities in this relationship. It's my house, too.

Ideally: My options would be: money to have an office suite near home to share with others.

DALE'S WANTS

I want the back bedroom for an office because:

I want a light-filled room to work in (dining room is too dark)

I want to be able to watch Kendra in the back yard.

I don't want to spend extra rent for an office.

Ideally: My options would be to work at home to be with Kendra and the back bedroom would make the best office.

Continue asking yourself the questions, and expanding your lists, until you feel you have gotten down to your most basic wants and options about the issue. Then share your lists. As you explore your underlying, more detailed wants in this step, enough new options should become clear to you that your apparent scarcity disappears, and you can go on to exploring options and deciding.

Don and Dale learned a lot about themselves and each other by exploring what they wanted, and the problems became less threatening, because they could see the reasons behind the wants, and understand each other's positions better. But they didn't feel that the apparent scarcity was completely gone. If exploring wants does not give you enough information, go on to the next step.

1. Expand the boundaries of the problem:

The purpose of this step is to help you remove any arbitrary and previously unnoticed restrictions or false limits you and your partner may have placed on the possible solutions to your problem. Answer the following questions as they relate to your apparent scarcity:

- Is there anything you have not considered doing, having, saying, or trying, because you don't think it's worth mentioning?
- How can you stretch your view of what's possible and what your resources are?
- Can you include more space, more time, other people, money you weren't thinking of before?
- Are there any rules you don't really need to obey?
- What are the limitations you are placing on the situation?

For Don and Dale, looking beyond the boundaries produced the following options:

Looking beyond the boundary of the back bedroom:

- use the dining room. convert the garage
- use the attic or the basement. add a room.
- get a motor home and set it up in the yard
- get a tent and set it up in the yard. move to a larger house.
- rent space nearby.
- reorganize the house, move our bedroom into the dining room, eat in the kitchen, and use both bedrooms for office space.
- both squeeze into the back bedroom, and pay Don's office rent into a building fund.
- Whoever gets the bedroom shares the cost for the other to rent an office outside.

In exploring their wants and expanding their boundaries, the partners learned a lot about each other and themselves, and can now see that a solution is not as impossible as they previously thought. Don and Dale have so many new and promising options that their problem should be quite easy to solve now.

Fred and Naomi's problem, being intangible and emotional, and involving sex, which is difficult for many people to talk about, could be more difficult to solve than Don and Dale's more mundane and concrete issue. But when they explored their wants and expanded their boundaries, they came up with the following ideas:

- Sex doesn't always have to be the same for both of us. Fred could masturbate, and Naomi could just hold him as he does.
- We could cuddle and watch erotic movies, so Fred can feel sexy, and Naomi can get affection.
- Affection can include holding hands, talking quietly, sending flowers, Naomi can ask Fred for whatever would make her feel safe whenever he makes a sexual overture.
- Fred and Naomi could go for sex therapy and find out more options.

Doing Research

Usually, when you have found an option you both like, it is easy to move forward to a decision to implement it to solve your problem. But sometimes an immediate solution isn't obvious, because more information is needed. For example:

- You may come up with a good idea, but you don't know if it will really work until you gather more facts.
- You may come up with an idea that you think will work, but you won't know until you try it.
- One partner may be delighted with an idea, but the other won't be sure until he or she sees what it's really like.

When this happens, you need to research either by gathering information or trying out your solution on a temporary basis.

If you still don't have enough information to resolve the problem, or you have questions (what are the legal issues? how will it feel to do something new? can we really live up to our agreement?) Setting up a research project will reassure you and give you the extra information you need. When Joe wasn't sure that having a housekeeper would work for him, he and Carol experimented by hiring a housecleaning service on a trial basis before making their final decision.

Research and Experimentation

The only way to find out if a solution (such as who does a particular household chore, how to handle a problem with your families the next time it comes up, a new sexual variation, or changing the set-up of your living room) will work is to try it on an experimental basis to see if it actually works before committing to a decision.

Gathering Information

If, when you have considered options, you find you have a lot of unanswered questions (how much will it cost? how long will it take? do we know enough to do it ourselves, or should we hire someone?) and need more facts before you'll know if a proposed solution is feasible, you can research by gathering information. Check with resources (look it up online, take a class or workshop, call local businesses, ask a lawyer, a doctor, a plumber, a travel agent, a mechanic or other expert, or ask friends or business associates who have tried whatever you want to know about) who have more information than you do about what you need to know. Divide up the research, then get back together and share what you've learned.

Guidelines for Doing Research

1. Agree to Research:

If you have questions about how your ideas will work, reaffirm that the purpose of the research is to get more information that will help both of you get your wants met. If one of you does not agree that research is a good idea at this point, use active listening, attentive speaking and I messages to find out why. If your partner is worried about something, reassure your partner what you would do if that happens. If the reluctance is due to something else, then treat it as a new problem to be negotiated.

2. Decide whether the type of research you do will be:

A. Experimentation

Try a solution for a limited period of time to see how it works, as Joe and Carol did when they hired a housekeeper on a trial basis for a month. To experiment, pick one of your possible solutions to try out.

Steps for Experimentation:

1. Set Time Limit:

Set a time limit for how long you'll try your experiment (Carol and Joe decided on one month) before you get back together and discuss the results. Limiting the time for the trial will reassure both of you that you haven't yet committed to a decision you're not sure of, and it will also make sure you don't forget to complete the negotiation.

2. Set Time and Place:

Set a meeting date after the experiment when you can discuss how the trial went, and whether the solution works or not. This provides the uninterrupted, unhurried time you need to discuss the results of your experiment, and complete your negotiation.

3. Conduct the Experiment:

Try your temporary solution for the specified time, with both of you paying attention to how well you think it works. The point is to get the experience to know if your solution is mutually satisfying. You may want to make notes to use in your discussion later, to ensure that you will be able to communicate the results of your experiment, how well you liked or didn't like it, and what you learned from it to each other.

Joe and Carol met after the housekeeper had been there several times, and Joe decided the housekeeping solution was fine with him. There was no privacy problem, because he wasn't home during that time. Carol loved the extra help, and was less tired after work, so she was more pleasant for Joe to be around, and they both decided the expense was well worth it, so they agreed that their problem was solved. If the trial had not solved their problem, they would have resumed brainstorming, using the new information they had from having tried the housekeeper.

4. Resume Negotiation:

After the trial period, meet at the specified time and place, and discuss the information you gained from your experiment. If your trial experiment seems to satisfy both of you, your problem is solved. If it doesn't work, resume exploring options and continue on through The Negotiation Tree.

B. Information Gathering.

Seek more facts and details about the solution, until you know how it works. Paul and Mary found out more about traveling by splitting the work: Paul searches for destinations online and Mary researches online travel sites to get more details and look up reviews. Together, they talk to friends who have traveled where they want to go.

Steps to Gather Information:

1. Divide Work:

Decide what information you need (Paul and Mary needed to know about cost of resorts, what resorts were in the mountains with lakes nearby, travel costs accommodations and reviews) and where it is available (online travel sites, friends) and divide up the work, as Paul and Mary did. One of you contacts half of the sources, the other contacts the rest.

2. Set Time and Place:

Set another meeting date when you can discuss the information you've gathered, and how it changes your ideas and your opinions of the possible solutions. This puts a time limit on how long you have to complete your research.

3. Gather Information:

Do whatever research you agreed on, take notes, gather pamphlets, articles, facts and figures as needed, and summarize what you've found out so that you can explain it to your partner. Paul and Mary brought info and prices to their meeting.

4. Resume Negotiation:

After your meeting, the new facts you've gathered will probably make it clear which option will satisfy both of you and your problem will be solved. If not, you may want to try an experiment or return to exploring options.

Deciding and Confirming Your Decision

Once you come up with a solution you can both agree on, it may seem the process is complete. But it's still possible for one or both of you to be confused or to differ in your understanding of what the decision is. Confirming the Decision is a skill that helps you verify that you both know what solution you've agreed to, so you can avoid three problems:

1. Silent disagreement:

One of you may feel the agreement places some undue burden on you, but you haven't let your reservations be known.

This is our old friend, the Rescue, coming up one last time, and causing you to not want to disappoint the partner who is excited about the option. As always, rescuing builds resentment, and you could find that the agreement you thought you made doesn't really work.

When Don and Dale discussed their new office situation, Don noticed he felt a little burdened and resentful, but he didn't say anything, because their negotiation had taken quite a long time, and he thought Dale might be upset if he objected. So, when the time came to move the offices, Don felt angry, irritable and uncooperative.

2. Different interpretations:

You and you partner may understand the agreement differently and inadvertently create different hidden expectations that will erupt later.

When Joe and Carol decided to try a housekeeper, they created some confusion:

Joe: OK, here's the agreement: We hire a housekeeper for a one-month trial period. See if we can get someone for $50 a day. Then we'll meet the first Saturday after the month is up and decide if we like it.

Carol: Good, I'll look for a housekeeper.

Carol did find one who charged $50 a day, and signed up for every Wednesday for one month. It wasn't until the fourth cleaning day that Joe realized she was coming weekly, when he thought she was going to come twice a month. He was dismayed to discover his cost was twice what he thought it was.

3. Unequal satisfaction:

You may not both feel equally satisfied and not realize it which can lead to one partner unconsciously sabotaging or not living up to the agreement.

Paul got really enthused about their vacation in the mountains, and decided a small, rustic lakeside resort in Washington state. Mary agreed at first, but later began to realize that the resort was not nearly as luxurious as she wanted, and she started complaining about something every time Paul mentioned the trip: the packing was difficult, the airline food would be lousy, and who would care for the cat while they were away. Mary's disappointment was causing her to unconsciously sabotage their plans.

When you formally decide on a solution, confirm and then finalize your decision, you avoid these problems.

Deciding

If you have laid the proper groundwork by exploring options until you have several good ones to choose from, brainstorming if you don't have enough, and experimenting or gathering information if you need more facts, deciding is usually very straight forward. Once you have enough possible solutions for the problem, at least one acceptable one will stand out to each of you. When you find a mutually satisfying decision, both of you will feel a sense of completion or relief.

When Joe and Carol had completed their decision about housework, Carol felt relieved and more relaxed when she thought she wouldn't have to deal with housecleaning and she had Joe's support and approval. Joe felt relieved, too, because he had felt pressured and guilty about not wanting to do his share. Their success was gratifying and they both felt full of goodwill and celebration. When you feel relieved, enthusiastic or satisfied when have come to your decision, you are ready to finalize your agreement:

Guidelines for Deciding

1. Choose your individual favorite:

From the options that you've developed on your abundance worksheet, through the brainstorming exercise, or through a research project, each of you choose separately the option that satisfies you. If you can't do this, go back to research and experimentation.

2. Share your choices:

Tell each other what your favorite choice is. If you've chosen the same one, your decision is made, and you can go on to Step 4. If you choose different options, go on to step three.

3. Try to combine choices:

Look for a way to combine your favorite choices, into one option that covers both of them.

Once Paul and Mary agreed on a mountain resort by a lake, Paul wanted a rustic resort, but Mary's choice was a more luxurious one. They found out they could combine those choices by choosing a resort in a wildlife preserve that had all the amenities of a fine hotel, including a lake and a pool, but had hiking, backpacking and fishing also available.

When you have found a suitable combination, move on to step four.

4. Check for relief:

Check with each other to see how you feel about the decision. Once your decision is made, you should both feel somewhat relieved, relaxed, and satisfied, and you can go on to confirming the decision. If you don't feel relieved or complete about your decision you need to brainstorm, use the abundance worksheet, or set up a research Project to generate more information.

When Don and Dale discussed their new office situation, Don noticed he felt a little burdened and resentful, and he realized their decision meant he was agreeing to a lot of work and responsibility so that he could have a new outside office. He discussed his reservations with Dale. As a result, they modified their decision to give Dale more of the setup work. At that point, the agreement felt much more equal to Don, and he felt relieved and happy to make the decision. Dale still felt he was getting what he wanted and was happy to make the adjustment.

If, like Don, you feel uneasy, confused or unsure, you may:

- Discuss your misgivings with your partner.
- Review the decision for flaws or omissions, and go back to brainstorming to develop more options or fine tune the ones you have.
- Decide to experiment with your decision to see if it works well. If you are experiencing some doubt and cannot figure out what it is, turn your best options into an experiment, using the guidelines for doing research.

Confirming the Decision

To confirm your decision, you both review it, and communicate your understanding of it to each other. If you don't confirm, you can create confusing and different expectations, as when Joe was dismayed to find out that they were paying for twice as much housekeeping time as he thought.

Guidelines for Confirming Your Decision

1. Repeat the decision:

In your own words, express your understanding of the decision you have reached. This allows you to make sure you've covered all the details, as well as a chance to imagine together how satisfactory your solution will be.

Each of you can share:

A. Understanding:

Your understanding of what the solution is, and how it will work: When Joe and Carol reconfirmed their decision about housework to clear up the confusion, Joe said, "As I understand it, we'll hire the housekeeper to come every other week, and we'll split the cost." Carol agreed.

B. Responsibility:

What you each expect to contribute to the solution: Joe and Carol would each pay half the cost,

C. Benefit:

How you will benefit from the solution: Joe and Carol both get a clean house, Carol will be less stressed, and Joe won't have to do housework.

Finalizing Your Agreement

When negotiation is new to you, or when your decision is complex, we recommend you avoid possible disagreement or unhappiness later by writing up a formal agreement that lists what you both feel you have decided on.

Verbal agreements can leave room for misunderstandings like Joe and Carol's, because you may skip over important details. Writing down your agreement minimizes these problems by revealing any obvious areas of misunderstanding about your decision and by forcing you to be clearer and more precise about the specifics of your agreement; and ensures that you both understand exactly what the agreement is. If you get confused later, you can check your written agreement to clear up the confusion.

Because they settled for a verbal agreement, Joe and Carol created confusion before, so this time they decided to write out their contract. Carefully written out, Joe and Carol's new contract read: We will hire the housekeeper to come one day, every other week, for a one-month trial period, at a cost of no more than $50 each time.

Once you become familiar with negotiation, it is usually sufficient to confirm your agreement in a few words informally stated. But when a problem is complex or longstanding, a written contract is always helpful in making sure your agreement is clear.

Guidelines for Finalizing Your Decision

1. Write out what you confirmed:

Write out your agreement in contract form, stating what each of you expects to contribute to and to gain from the agreement, as in these examples:

Don and Dale's written contract read: Don will temporarily move his office into the dining room to save money and Dale will move his into the back bedroom. They will both ask friends to see who would like to share an outside office rental with Don. Don will look for suitable office space to rent, and Dale will share the moving expenses and renovation work (painting, shelves, moving furniture, installing phones, etc.) for Don to move into the house and back out again later. When enough money is saved, Don will move into his shared office with friends, and Dale will still have his office in the back bedroom.

John and Mary's contract read: Mary will go back to school with

John's full encouragement and support. Mary will continue to support John with executive dinners and parties and running errands when necessary, and John agrees to give her enough notice and to accommodate her school schedule (no surprise dinner guests the night before a test).

2. *Read and sign:*

Read your written agreement out loud, and sign it to signify your bargain. Once you've done this, your agreement is finalized, unless circumstances change.

3. *Renegotiation*

Even when you both feel sure your solution is perfect, circumstances may change, requiring a change in your solution. No couple can foresee all possible events, and any solution that works today may be obsolete tomorrow.

If Don were offered an excellent job, he might give up his business, making an office unnecessary, or if someone fell ill in the family, Mary and Paul might decide to use their vacation time to help out, and shelve their vacation plans. Or, one of you might decide that an agreement is no longer working for you. Therefore, all solutions need to be renegotiable at any time. To honor your commitment to each other's satisfaction, any solution must be renegotiable if either of you becomes unhappy with it.

As Rose and John grow older, their circumstances may change (retirement, new interests.) Don and Dale eventually had thriving businesses, and a whole suite of offices.

Problems like illness, reduction of income, or an acquired handicap can arise, or you may just grow tired of the way you are doing things. Cooperating means working together to find new solutions if old solutions no longer work for one or both of you.

Don and Dale were well along in carrying out their agreement when Don found out that one of his co-renters dropped out and another wanted to delay moving in for six more weeks, which made the rent too much. Don asked Dale to negotiate a modification in their time schedule (which would also affect their financial agreement), and they were able to renegotiate a six-week extension to the original plan.

Guidelines for Successful Renegotiation

1. State that it's renegotiable:

Adding the phrase "all solutions are renegotiable at any time" to all your agreements removes the pressure to make the solution perfect for all possible outcomes, and reassures both of you that you can always renegotiate.

2. Don't make unilateral changes:

Renegotiate your agreements instead of breaking or deviating from them. You and your partner will never be able to trust any of your agreements if you can break it anytime it becomes inconvenient or unpleasant for you. Renegotiating makes sure no one is surprised, betrayed or deceived, and enhances the trust between you.

3. Repeat the negotiation process:

Let your partner know whenever a solution isn't working for you, and why, and formally request a renegotiation.

4. Emergency Procedure:

If an emergency occurs (my car caught fire on a business trip, you weren't home when I called) and you are forced to break an agreement (I had to spend the money we were saving for our vacation to fix the car) without renegotiating, formally acknowledge that you broke the pact, explain why it was an emergency, and apologize, then renegotiate the original agreement to cover such emergencies.

5. Slight modifications:

If you are only seeking to modify your agreement slightly, your renegotiation may be as simple as setting the stage and considering other options:

Paul and Mary agreed on Lake Tahoe for their vacation, but Paul later became concerned about the cost and wanted to consider reducing expenses. They decided on a less expensive hotel in a few minutes.

6. Changing Longstanding agreements:

If the agreement you want to renegotiate is a basic or longstanding one, you may need to follow The Negotiation Tree from the beginning:

When John's retirement became imminent, he and Rose spent considerable time and care in negotiating their new arrangement to accommodate his retirement and Rose's new career.

There is one more equally vital step: Celebrate what you have both accomplished by working together to solve your problem.

Celebration

Our detailed instructions can make negotiating seem complicated and drawn-out, but with practice, each of the steps of The Negotiation Tree will become easier until they seem natural to you, and you won't have to give it very much thought. Every negotiation will then be successful, and an opportunity for a celebration. Most people have a tendency to give more attention to what doesn't work than what does work and so they never give themselves a chance to acknowledge and savor success.

Celebrating the successful completion of your cooperative negotiation accomplishes many things:

- Celebration acknowledges and establishes in your minds that you've accomplished a satisfying end to what may have been a difficult problem,
- Celebration helps you focus on the good feelings you have about each other,
- Celebration produces what psychologists call a sense of closure: a clear concluding moment and a feeling of resolution to your diligent work, so that no residual resentment remains.
- Celebration makes you focus attention on the positive result of

your negotiation, when it might be easy to put most of your energy on the negative.

- Celebration provides a moment of warmth and goodwill, the hallmarks of happy partnership.
- Celebration is a reward for work well done, and also creates motivation for future cooperative negotiation.
- Celebration will motivate you to continue cooperating and solving problems as a team.

Guidelines for Celebration

1. Suggest a Celebration:

End each successful negotiation by saying: "We did it! Now how do you want to celebrate?" Design your celebration to fit your accomplishment, and to have fun.

2. Create a Celebration Guide:

Develop a list of the items or activities that really mean celebration to both of you:

- balloons,
- champagne or sparkling cider,
- friends or family around,
- use the best dishes,
- a barbecue in the yard go out somewhere nice to eat,
- get pizza,
- get tickets to a show,
- go to the movies,
- greeting cards,
- post on social media,
- make love,
- bake cookies,
- call someone to share the good news, or
- simply congratulate each other on a job well done.

Over a period of time together, you can develop a list of celebration items and activities that you can use as a resource each time you want to celebrate success.

After Don found two friends to share an office suite with him and found reasonably priced, attractive space to share, he and Dale celebrated their decision three times. First, they got a sitter for Kendra and went out to dinner to their favorite restaurant. Then, they got together with the co-renters and had cake and coffee to celebrate and seal the deal. Finally, Don and his friends had an office warming party, at which Don made a speech acknowledging Dale for his help in coming up with the idea and helping to bring it all together.

Paul and Mary celebrated their decision to go to Lake Tahoe on an excursion deal by hugging and sending out for a pizza at the end of their negotiation, and then, at a special dinner during their vacation, they made a champagne toast to each other for being such smart negotiators. When they came home, they posted vacation shots on social media, and also bragged to their friends about how they had the best vacation of their lives, and that negotiation had helped them accomplish it.

Joe and Carol celebrated their decision to experiment with a housekeeper by eating takeout food on paper plates and throwing them away, so no one had to do any dishes.

John and Rose, whose decision was made after they stated their wants, celebrated by making love, and telling each other how much they appreciated their mutual caring and their communication.

As a couple, you now have the basic tools you need for co-creating your ideal relationship. Because these skills, techniques and attitudes are new and somewhat revolutionary compared to the way most people think relationships work, you will need to practice them: start with simple problems or purposely easy problems such as who takes out the trash or what the schedule for using the bathroom will be. Simple problems give you the greatest chance of success, and time to practice before you handle more difficult problems. Keep The Negotiation Tree handy for your first few negotiations to help you remember what step you are on, prevent you from skipping vital steps, and refer you back to sections in the book if you get stuck along the way.

As your familiarity with cooperative negotiation increases, you will be able to handle more difficult problems. As you practice, your skills will improve until you can handle your most emotional disagreements and complex problems without resorting to arguing or fighting.

If something comes up that you cannot handle through negotiation, you'll know that you need help from a marriage counselor or other expert and the attempts you made at solving the problem cooperatively will save you time and money in counseling by clarifying where and how you are stuck. Often, a problem that you have discussed by negotiating can be solved in one counseling session, because the groundwork is already done.

Your new skills in cooperative negotiation make it possible to work out anything that troubles you, and even things that don't. Using these techniques, you can change your way of being together, creating more comfort that feels great to both of you. Your relationship will be satisfying, sustainable, and you will feel happy in your partnership.

Chapter Seven

Creating Happy Partnership

To create a happy partnership, it is necessary to honor each other's personalities, emotional needs, circumstances (such as family situations, financial realities, careers, and children) and your willingness to do what you agree to. Happy partnerships have room for fun, hard work and rest. Happy partners understand that if either of them is deprived, too stressed or overloaded, the relationship will suffer.

Once you solve the day-to-day problems you can use cooperation and negotiation to shape and create a truly sustainable, cooperative partnership that is tailor made to your individual personalities and meets both of your needs to a degree you may not have dreamed possible. What makes it possible is that you have a method for both of you to get what you want all the time every time.

Barriers to Happy Partnership

The areas where couples usually have the greatest number of problems are:

- Romance: Expectations of reproducing the attractive, dramatic and perfect results depicted in movies and television can lead to setting up ideals that are impossible to attain, and create inevitable disillusionment and a sense of failure.
- Lovemaking: In a society where sexuality is both suppressed

and over exaggerated, and where the models presented in fiction are almost always based on the excitement of first love, you and your partner may have no idea how sexuality works in long-term, committed relationships, or how to keep your sexual excitement alive.

- Personality quirks: All of us have individual behaviors and needs that vary from what our partners were raised to believe were acceptable; and these can produce major struggles when we do not know how to effectively resolve and solve conflicts.

- Good times and bad times: The natural ups and downs of life, such as illness, financial stress, major business success, or parenting issues, have a strong impact on your relationship, and if you do not know how to tough changes you may not know how to handle the good fortunes either.

- Transitions: Moving gracefully through the years and from one stage of life to another does not always come naturally. When either of you are struggling with these transitions, you may be out of sorts, which leads to conflict and disagreement.

- Forgiveness: No two people can spend extended time together without making mistakes, hurting feelings or making each other angry. If you do not know how to set these feelings aside and forgive yourself and your partner, this anger festers and grows until it smothers the fires of love that brought you together.

- Challenges: If you have old, unresolved pain from childhood events or past relationships, the unhealed emotional wounds can create overreactions to normal relationship problems and challenges of life. Such feelings can be overwhelmingly negative and make the problem seem unsolvable, causing serious relationship damage.

All of these barriers to sustainable happy partnership can be overcome using problem solving skills. You and your partner can become happy partners by honoring each other's personalities, emotional needs, circumstances (such as family situations, financial realities, career demands and the needs of children) individual quirks, foibles, faults and problems. The steps of The Negotiation Tree ensure that you have methods of confronting and overcoming all these factors when your work together to solve the related problems.

Romance

When you commit to your relationship and live together for an extended period of time, the initial excitement and newness eventually wears off, and the heightened energy and excitement of being together that we call romance lessens because you begin to get into a familiar day-to-day routine. This is actually a good thing, and it means you're doing OK.

When you live separately and date each other, being apart heightens the drama and excitement of being together. Getting ready for a date, showering, shaving and dressing, becomes a slow, steady buildup of excitement. Every time you see each other is special, romantic.

From the moment you begin to live together, this buildup to romance and specialness ceases to exist. Romantic moments are no longer automatically a part of being together. Instead, much of your time together is spent on more mundane things: doing laundry, washing dishes, paying bills, childcare, home maintenance, or going to work. After the newness of living together wears off, these things cease to feel romantic, and you may worry that your partner no longer cares as much or is as excited to be with you.

Experts know that this change is good: Romance is based on fantasy but lasting love is grounded in reality. Real life love requires real people who can be there to support each other through tough periods like grief, upsets, and financial setbacks, as well as to share good times and the joy of success.

Viewed this way, romance becomes a very useful tool you can use in conjunction with negotiation to renew the energy in your relationship, whenever you feel the need. By using your skills in communicating what you want, agreeing to negotiate and exploring options to solve the problem of lack of romance or excitement between you, you can figure out how to celebrate your love, affection and desire for each other, which will remind and reassure both of you that you are special to each other.

When you feel the energy between you needs a recharge, you can become purposeful about romance. When you affirm your love and connection, you remind each other that you are special by arranging a date, a present, a surprise, a joke or a hug as needed.

These romantic events could include:

- Arranging a date, a present, a surprise, a joke or a hug when your emotional connection needs reinforcement.
- Meeting at a singles bar, pretending to pick each other up, and winding up the evening at a hotel.
- Acting out fantasies: photographer and model, movie star couple, nurse and doctor, stripper and audience member.
- Taking a special vacation to a romantic spot together.
- Setting aside one evening a week for a date and doing what you used to do when you first met.
- Spending a weekend morning having breakfast in bed.
- Sending a card, a plant, flowers, cologne, or other present by messenger or leaving them as a surprise on a day that's not normally a gift-giving occasion.
- Take a class together in something new and fun like mountain climbing, dancing, skiing, acting, roller-skating, pottery making, painting, stained glass, sailing, swimming, auto mechanics or cooking or get involved in the community to create new experiences together.

What feels romantic and loving to you may or not be similarly effective for your partner, so the first step to creating romance becomes figuring out and sharing what is romantic to each of you. The following exercise will help you do that.

Exercise: Creating Romance

Each of you answer the following questions, then discuss and compare your answers.

1. Recall romantic scenes:

What is romantic to you? Think back to the most passionate or romantic times of your life, the most romantic scenes in movies, TV shows, books or plays. List them like this:

- The heroine awakens to find the hero filled her house with flowers.
- The couple holds hands and watches the sunset.
- Couples greet each other at airports.
- She taunts him through the glass door, he breaks in and they make love.

1. Analyze for meaning:

What excites you about this? Review these romantic scenes and analyze them for what made them seem passionate, exciting or romantic.

- Flowers and thoughtful surprises seem romantic to me.
- Being so comfortable and at ease with each other, taking time together, seems romantic.
- Getting together after separation is romantic
- Being turned on enough to struggle to get to me is passionate and exciting.

2. Create your own version:

What (perhaps simplified) realistic versions of these romantic scenes could you create in your relationship?

- Surprise each other with cards, gifts, flowers. It doesn't have to be expensive to be thoughtful.
- Set aside quiet time to spend together.
- Greet each other like you've been apart when you come home from work
- Let each other know when you're turned on, even at times that

might not be convenient. Figure out how to tease each other a little: Make a sexy phone call at work; put a naughty picture or a flower in your partner's briefcase.

3. Talk about turn-ons and romance:

Discuss your lists, looking for similarities and differences in what you like and dislike. Your partner's list provides clues to how you can easily create a romantic mood he or she will respond to, and your own list will help you get yourself into a romantic mood. The most successful mutually romantic moments will include elements from each of your lists.

Keep these lists of romantic possibilities to use as resources whenever you want to create a romantic moment together. Using romance and fantasy in this way, to spice up selected moments of your life together, instead of holding unrealistic and fantastic expectations of what your relationship should be like, keeps your relationship fun, exciting and unpredictable enough to be interesting, but also possible for you to sustain without stress.

Lovemaking

Closely related to romance, but much more reality-based, is sexual intimacy, another area where unrealistic expectations can lead to hurt and disappointment.

In long-term relationships, lovemaking is different than it is for new couples, whose passion is often built on the excitement of the new and unknown. For a couple who have been together for years, there is not much unknown, so the energy for lovemaking must be derived elsewhere.

When things go well, the passion of a new, exciting sexual relationship is transmuted over the years into a deep, warm, sensual connection that also has a sense of humor. If you allow your lovemaking to change and grow, rather than holding to rigid expectations or getting stuck in repetitive patterns, it will change and grow, as you do, and as your partnership does.

This openness to what is happening right now, and responsiveness to each other and the moment, is actually what you did when you were new to each other. A significant part of passion is the exploration of the unknown. What we often lose sight of when we've been together for several years, is that there is still an unknown to be explored. By remaining open to the changes in each other, and by remembering to approach each other as interesting, growing and changing people, you can keep the sense of passion alive for a lifetime.

On the other hand, one of the true joys of sexual intimacy with a long-term, beloved and well-known partner is the comfort and ease of knowing what your lover enjoys, and receiving pleasure from a partner who is experienced in what you like.

Sexual Repertoire

The most helpful tool to sustain sexuality over a long relationship is a sexual repertoire: several varieties of sexual encounter to cover different times in the relationship.

For example, Jay and Pat have a joke about having "microwave sex, for when we're too tired to cook" This means that when they would like to be close and sexual, but are too tired to cook (get very excited and hot), they get out the electric appliances: vibrators can make the foreplay part of sexuality easy and effortless, allowing them to have sex in the easiest possible way.

There's also romantic sex, for the times when you are on vacation, or have a special evening or afternoon together, complete with flowers, fine dining, dressing up, or whatever spells romance to you.

Or, there's quickie sex, for those times when your time is short (you only have a few minutes before work), when you skip the fine points, use a lubricant to speed things up, and have sex the quickest way possible.

The possible varieties of sexual attitudes, environments, energies and activities are truly endless. The most important thing is that you not get stuck in any one pattern, but allow yourselves a variety of sexual expression.

The following exercise will help open your communication about sexual varieties and patterns:

Exercise: Sexual Variety

Use the following list to get you started in a discussion of different sexual possibilities and your feelings and desires. Consider each item on the following list, and imagine what each type of sex might be for you. Then discuss your answers and then follow through by trying out a few of your favorite ideas. If you get stuck, a Sexual Communication Exercise is below.

What are your ideas about:

- Sex when you're too tired
- Sex when you're uptight
- Sex when you're uninspired
- Sex when you're all right
- Quickies: sex in a rush
- Sex on special occasions
- Silly Sex
- Sneaky Sex (getting around kids, in-laws, the boss)
- Romantic Sex (see special occasions)
- Newlywed Sex (like we used to do it)
- Making-up Sex
- Comforting Sex
- Healing Sex (sex when you're sick or grieving)
- Relaxing Sex (slow, lazy, no pressure)
- Reassuring Sex (affection and intimacy intended to reassure a partner who is temporarily insecure, or for reaffirming your mutual interest)
- Generous Sex (to make your partner happy)
- Selfish Sex (all for yourself)
- Fantasy Sex (playacting, dressing up, and so forth)

When you work together to make each other happy, you create an attitude of openness and responsiveness to each other and the moment, that will remind you of the way you approached lovemaking when you were new to each other.

Sexual Communication

Your sexual relationship is another avenue of communication; whatever is going on in the rest of your lives will be reflected sexually. Any distance or blocked communication between you will be demonstrated in your bedroom.

The problem-solving techniques and communication skills you have learned in this book will help you keep your sexuality alive and pleasurable. A sexual problem can be solved like any other problem, by communicating about it and exploring solutions.

Here's a brief guideline to help you discuss sexual differences, wants, confusion, and to help you improve your understanding of each other's sexual needs. It's OK to disagree or have different ideas. Focus on learning about each other, and find ways to meet both of your wants whenever possible.

Exercise: Sexual Communication

Answer the following questions, then discuss and compare your answers:

1. What I like about our lovemaking now is…
2. What I miss that we used to do when we first met is…
3. I would like more….
4. I would like less….
5. I'm worried that you feel…
6. I want to feel more…
7. I'm afraid, as we stay together longer, we will…
8. In ten more years, I would like our lovemaking to be…

Enjoyable sex does not happen automatically as the years go by; you need to discuss and negotiate it like all other aspects of your relationship. Use your negotiating skills when sexual problems or differences arise, and you'll be able to keep good, satisfying (and frequently great) sex as an integral part of your sustainable relationship, for as long as you both want to.

Personality Quirks

You and your partner are different in background, experience and early training, so each of you has small quirks, personality traits or habits that must be accommodated, in one way or another, if you want a sustainable relationship.

Over time these quirks (like a laugh that grates on your nerves, differences in messiness or neatness, irritating jokes or stories, incompatible work schedules, different ideas about housekeeping, your partner's nail-biting or smoking, what and when to feed the dog, how politely to speak to your children, or how warm the room should be) can feel like sufficient reason to get a divorce.

Many of these things may seem silly or embarrassing to bring up, but if you can't negotiate and resolve your frustrations they can become a serious problem.

Guidelines for Resolving Irritation

1. Don't sweat it:

Sometimes, your partner's quirks, such as being messy, picking at teeth, not putting lids back on jars tightly, watching TV too much, or singing off key, are small enough to be easily dismissed by deciding the whole package of your partner more than makes up for the little annoying habits.

If you can do this without resentment, your partner's quirks will cease to be a problem.

2. Voluntarily change:

Each of you can also voluntarily modify your own behavior (go to the bathroom to pick teeth, screw the lids on tight) to reduce the annoyance to your partner.

3. Distract yourself:

You can minimize (by leaving the room or distracting yourself with a project) the impact of your partner's habits on yourself.

4. Negotiate about it:

If the above three steps don't work, and you feel irritated and resentful about a quirk or habit, you and your partner discuss the problem objectively, without blame or defensiveness, to create solutions that satisfy both of you.

Exercise: Discussing Quirks

Answer the following questions; discuss them as in the prior exercises:

1. Irritations:

List the little habits that irritate you most about your partner:
- squeezes toothpaste tube wrong
- spends too much time in bathroom
- is messy in the kitchen

2. Partner's irritation:

List your own personal habits that irritate your partner:
- smoking
- messy piles of papers

3. Review:

Consider your answers to question 1 and list any items you want to negotiate.

4. Compare lists:

Imagine that you are doing a scene in a comedy television show, and see if you can feel the humor in your situation. If you can laugh about your own quirks and your irritation at your partner's weird habits, discussing and resolving your differences about them will be much easier. When comparing your lists, you'll find that some things you were annoyed about will fade away just by discussing them, and others will seem unimportant after being explained.

5. Negotiate:

At the end of your discussion, make a date to negotiate whatever is left on your lists from step three, and use your negotiation skills to resolve them.

Good Times, Bad Times

As a couple, you will go through good times and bad times, and probably face fights, tragedies, betrayal, and struggle in a lifetime of living together. Naturally you want to live happily ever after, and avoid facing the harder facts: What happens if you lose your job? How are we going to handle it if we have money difficulties? What if one of us gets very sick? What if you have a lot more success at your career than I do at mine? What if we get more successful than we ever dreamed? If you avoid talking about these possibilities, you won't feel prepared to handle them if they come up.

In a lifetime of living together, you and your partner need to be able to handle many ups and downs:

- Problems to solve and victories to celebrate
- Moments of excitement and moments of peace.
- Times of boredom and times of stressful activity
- Peaks of tremendous love and caring for each other, and valleys of distance and irritation.
- Fights and harmonious times
- Tragedies and blessed events

You can be prepared to meet all these ups and downs as a team, work together to solve the problems, and celebrate your successes. Each time you demonstrate that you are a team who can remain calm in times of crisis, think problems through carefully, solve them in a way that satisfies both of you, and enjoy your successes to the fullest you will strengthen your bond of trust and partnership, and feel blessed and happy in your relationship.

The trick is to learn to live it all as fully as possible, accept it as much as you can (resisting the hard times doesn't make them go away, it just makes handling them tougher) to learn from experience, correct mistakes, solve the problems, keep your lines of communication open, and don't take it too seriously. With your communication and negotiation skills, you can meet all these times as a team, work together to solve the problems, and wind up with a good, solid, and loving partnership.

Transitions

As time passes and you gain experience, your attitudes, expectations and preferences change, and your relationship must change as you do to be sustainable.

Whether these changes are caused by circumstances (a new job in a new city), personal growth (you grow more self-assured, and want to try new things), or an unexpected event (a serious illness) they always create some turmoil and confusion.

One way to help understand the changes is to see them in terms of growth. Your relationship will go through stages of growth, just as you will as an individual.

Growth Stages of a Relationship

1. Romance:

This is the exciting, passionate and unrealistic beginning of a new relationship, a head start that propels you together and excites and enthralls you enough to get through the early testing and power struggle phases. When this stage goes well, it provides incentive to go deeper into intimacy, but it doesn't last. Every successful relationship moves on to stage two.

2. Early commitment:

In this testing stage, you and your partner try to figure out if you are a good match. Unfortunately, if you have unrealistic expectations you may not use this stage effectively, because of fear that the testing means something's wrong. But, if the early, tentative testing goes well, you will be encouraged to let the relationship grow further.

3 Power struggle and conflict:

At this stage, the testing turns into conflict as you begin to work out how, and whether, each of you can be yourself while being partners. This is the most difficult stage for many people, and relationships often end here, because lovers with unrealistic expectations see this conflict as tragic rather than growth-producing. Couples who can negotiate as partners can be excited rather than overwhelmed by this challenge.

4. Resolution and Acceptance:

This is stage of practicality, where you've understood your limitations as individuals and accepted the hard work of listening, understanding the differences between the two of you, changing what can be changed, accepting what can't be, and making decisions. When you have good problem-solving skills, in this stage you can reach an agreement that works, and your partnership deepens and grows strong.

5. Commitment or ethical love:

At this stage, often a few years into the relationship, you make a commitment based on the realities, rather than on the excitement of new love.

6. Love made visible or mature romanticism:

Here you've reached the result of clarifying your values and priorities based on the assumption that you are committed to partnership and are willing to do whatever you can to help each other fulfill your potential.

At this stage you are happy partners, a team who can pull together in the same harness. Through experience and effort, you have built a sustainable relationship.

Going through relationship six stages can be difficult, and you won't necessarily progress neatly from one to the next, or find a stage where you can live happily ever after. Your happy partnership will continue to change and grow, and you'll meet various challenges at different times. Each of you can even be at different stages at the same time, but, if you accept the reality of your responsibility to keep the relationship healthy, the rewards are worth it.

These changes in the familiar way of doing things can cause uneasiness; but because you know how, these transitions can become just a series of problems you must solve.

When John and Rose made the transition to John's retirement, they faced many new problems:

- How their finances would change on John's fixed retirement income.

- What John would do to keep active and involved now that he had a lot of unstructured time, and felt useless and lost.

- Whether to stay in their large house (designed for raising children) or sell it and move to a condominium, or senior living

- What limits to set on babysitting for their grandchildren,

- How Rose's new career would be affected by John's retirement,

- How much traveling they would do together, where and in what way.

As they solved each of these problems individually, instead of viewing the whole thing as one big retirement problem, John and Rose were able to work out a balance between her career and his retirement that allowed them both to feel active and useful while still allowing them to enjoy leisure time and traveling.

You and your relationship will continue to grow and change and you won't always progress neatly from one stage to the next, or find an arrangement that is permanently satisfying. Each of you can even be at different stages at the same time! But, as you work together to resolve your new ways of doing things, and cooperate when differences come up, you'll soon learn to see each transition as an exciting new adventure or challenge instead of a frightening change.

The Transition to Parenting

The biggest transition any couple is becoming parents. Even if you and your partner look forward eagerly to your first child you will experience baby shock: the disorientation and dismay of dealing with the reality, rather than the fantasy, of having a baby. Couples who are surprised to be pregnant may be even more upset. A baby changes everything about your life: sleep schedules, priorities, your social life, your financial status, and the primary couple relationship. These changes happen overnight, because the day a baby is born, everything is different from the day before.

There is no way to accurately predict how these changes will feel, and the learning curve for new parents is very steep. The details of parenting are beyond the scope of this book, and there are many guides to help you deal with all these changes. When you decide to become parents knowing how to work together to solve problems will become precious to you, because you'll have tool to handle all of these massive changes, one at a time.

Forgiveness

As your relationship progresses, you will invariably fail to meet all of each other's expectations in some way. In a lifetime of living together, you are bound to hurt each other's feelings, betray trust, or let each other down from time to time, usually without intending to.

For example, if your mother was a wonderful cook, you may assume that your partner will cook what you like, or will like what you cook. Then, when that does not turn out to be the case, you may feel very disappointed and even resentful. If you don't discuss your food preferences, and you don't forgive each other, you could have a very serious problem. Such mutual resentment over small disappointments can lead to major relationship difficulty.

Some emotional hurts, such as when harsh words are spoken in anger and frustration, or when an illicit affair occurs during a relationship crisis, will only be resolved through healing and forgiveness. Negotiation will help you to forgive, because once you solve the problem and are sure you won't be hurt again, it is much easier to let go of the hurt feelings and get back on good terms with each other.

If you find you are holding hurt, anger or resentment toward your partner, first use the Problem Inventory exercise in Chapter Five until you understand clearly enough to communicate what the problem is that needs to be resolved. Then proceed to solve whatever you feel hurt or angry about as if it were any other problem. You'll find that once the problem is solved to your satisfaction, forgiving your partner (and yourself) is easier because the problem won't be repeated.

Challenges

Every relationship carries challenges to heal and grow, and because you and your partner are so intimately involved, your relationship is automatically an environment where old hurts and wounds from the past will arise. In fact, often we challenge each other in the very areas where we are wounded and most need to heal.

It is so common for couples with corresponding unfinished issues to get together (a woman with an alcoholic father falls for a heavy drinker, a man whose mother was absent or distant is attracted to cold, withdrawn women) that intimate, committed relationships often become arenas for facilitating healing and growth.

If painful events happened in your childhood, such as physical or verbal abuse, incest, rape, the loss or death of a parent or sibling, or a severe injury or illness, a relatively mild incident could cause you to unexpectedly relive the pain of your early trauma.

If you or your partner had very painful past relationships (battering, cheating, lying, abandonment, or severe financial damage) you can also carry unhealed psychological wounds which may cause you to overreact to unrelated problems in a current relationship.

Even when you are trying to be loving, as partners you can unintentionally recreate old painful scenes from childhood or previous relationships which become challenges you must overcome if you don't want this relationship to contain the same problems those old relationships had. The following exercises will help you.

Exercise: Overcoming Challenges

Part One: Challenge Indicator Checklist

If either of you is overreacting to the problems because of old, unresolved hurt and trauma from childhood or a past relationship, you will see one or more of the following indicators:

1. Stonewalling:

You can't or won't discuss a particular topic, such as a gambling problem, a difficult in-law, sexual dissatisfaction, or disciplining the children.

2. Repeating problems:

A problem seems unsolvable or recurs, such as a partner's unreliability or lateness, a struggle over money, or jealousy.

3. Unresolved arguing:

You argue about different topics, but all arguments sound, feel and end the same: For example, you both yell until one of storms out, or you don't speak for three days.

4. Attempts to negotiate end in arguments:

Even though you're used to working things out, you can't negotiate about a particular topic, because you end up arguing.

5. Blaming and Accusing:

One of you makes accusations including the words "you always" or "you never", indicating stored frustration, resentment and anger about something the other does or doesn't do.

6. Hopelessness:

You feel highly critical, hopeless, angry or resentful about your partner's traits or you become obsessed with making your partner see his or her problem and change it.

Part Two: Guidelines for Overcoming Challenges

Whenever any of the above indicators challenge your relationship or you feel one of them is threatening to disrupt or destroy your partnership, you can use the following steps to overcome it:

1. Don't panic:

As painful and overwhelming as they may seem, challenges are common in relationships and can be overcome with discussion and negotiation. Do your best to stay calm and use your listening and active speaking to find out as much as you can about what the problem is, and follow The Negotiation Tree as you would with any problem. If you can't stay calm enough to do that, go to step five

2. Develop temporary solutions:

Use the Guidelines for Doing Research in Chapter Six to develop temporary solutions such as agreeing to call a time out when issues get too heated. At the same time, work separately using the How to Set Aside Held Anger and Hurt exercise in Chapter Four.

If necessary, work with a therapist on resolving the trauma or wounds from the past that are evoked by situations in your relationship.

3. Be as supportive as you can:

If your partner is working on a challenge issue, do your best to be emotionally positive and encouraging. Reassure each other that you won't go away or avoid the issue. If the issue creates problems so difficult (violent outbursts, alcohol or drug addiction, severe sexual problems, emotional breakdowns) that you have to separate to protect yourself, you can still let your partner know you'd be willing to resume relationship once the problem is handled.

4. Get outside support:

Develop trustworthy friends, clergy or family members who can support you both emotionally while you overcome the challenge, and don't hesitate to let them know when you need help. Having someone who cares, and who can listen and support without interfering, will relieve some stress and help you stay calm so you can use your negotiation skills.

5. Get professional help:

If you have used the above four steps and your communication skills and the problem still seems overwhelming; especially if one or both of you has a history of abuse, alcohol problems, rape or incest, get professional help. A therapist is expert in just such issues, and can give you the objective, supportive feedback you need.

Understanding the signs that indicate challenges, knowing that they exist to varying degrees in most relationships, learning to take care of yourself, recognizing that challenges present an opportunity to heal and grow, and knowing when to get help will increase your ability to overcome challenges and keep them from permanently damaging your partnership.

Overcoming challenges and crises through working together will strengthen your bond of confidence and trust in each other and in your partnership.

The Power of Goal Setting

When you have a clear vision of your personal and relationship goals (if we save money we can have our own business), all your mutual decisions can be made with your overall goals in mind (we'll choose a less expensive vacation to save money). By working together to discover your mutual goals, you will gain a deeper understanding of your own as well as your partner's hopes and dreams, and the process of setting those goals together will help you know each other better. The love and mutual support you demonstrate to each other as you work together over the years becomes your solid foundation, free from held anger, resentment and hurt, which will reassure you in difficult times and make your joyful times more satisfying.

When you hesitate to discuss your hopes and dreams because you are concerned it will not go well, sharing a vision of the future seems futile. Because you have mastered communication and negotiation skills, you will discover that accommodating divergent goals deepens your bond and commitment and adds zest to your partnership.

Exercise: Setting and Achieving Goals

As a couple, you can set:

- emotional goals (to make weekends more fun and loving, to share feelings more often),
- financial goals (to save to buy a house),
- time goals (to have more time alone together)
- health goals (to go to gym together three times a week, to eat a more low-fat diet);
- sexual goals (to take a class in Tantric Yoga, to make time for sex at least twice a week, to experiment with a vibrator)
- career goals (to put one of you through school, to start a business together)
- social goals (to start a sports team, to help the homeless)
- recreational goals (to go on vacation, to relax more on weekends)

To set your partnership goals, use communication and negotiation to resolve any differences and create a workable, mutually satisfying purpose you wish to accomplish. Then follow these steps:

1. Set your intention:

Once you know what you want, you need to agree to go for it. The combination of desire and determination give you the direction and energy to act on your own behalf. Using the confirming your decision step of The Negotiation Tree (Chapter Six) can help you make sure your intention is mutual.

2. Break it down:

Break your purpose down into small steps that feel possible to accomplish, and list them. For example, if you have saved a down payment and want to buy a house, you could break that down into steps such as:

1. look online to find available houses in your chosen neighborhood;
2. find a realtor;
3. look at houses with the realtor
4. make a choice and an offer.

1. Divide the steps:

Decide who will do which steps. If it is not immediately obvious, use communication and negotiation to decide who does what. In the process of negotiating, you may find that either the steps or your stated purpose may change a bit.

2. Do something:

Obviously, you won't achieve your goal if you never get around to doing anything. Breaking your goal down into small steps should help you feel less overwhelmed and more motivated. However, if you find that you are not doing what you agreed to, go back to guideline two and break the goal into smaller, easier steps or use your active listening and attentive speaking skills (Chapter Three) to find out what is in the way.

3. Celebrate:

Many people focus more attention on what they have not accomplished than on what they have achieved. This is discouraging and can create a lack of enthusiasm. Celebrating the completion of each small step and appreciating yourself and each other for what you've done so far will motivate you and create energy to do more, because all of us feel more energized when we feel appreciated.

By setting your intention, creating small steps, and completing and celebrating each step of your plan as you go along, you'll find that you have changed your relationship in the desirable ways you want, and that even the work of creating change has been fun. After a few goal-setting successes, you'll find that your sense of commitment and confidence in your future is growing stronger.

Sustainability

You and your partner want to create a relationship that lasts. "I'll love you forever" is a promise that may be unrealistic and impossible to fulfill because it is based on fantasy. It's difficult to predict how you'll feel in five years, never mind forever.

While it's romantic and pleasant to speak about love, the true commitment in a healthy relationship is a dedication to mutuality, respect and fairness, because these activities increase and maintain the warmth in your relationship, which is the best guarantee of relationship commitment and sustainability.

To make a healthy commitment to having children or making long-term investments and decisions, you and your partner need to be able to thoroughly discuss decisions before they are made, and discuss future possibilities. For example, If you want a baby, you consider your competence as parents, take classes and babysitting for friends to learn more, and your financial responsibility, and you'll research the realities of child-rearing, You both realize that these serious decisions require serious thought, and that you are not taking care of yourselves (or your future children) if you decide based on fantasy ("Wouldn't it be nice to have a baby? Babies are so sweet and loveable") alone.

To be healthy in your relationship you need to value honest communication, so you are unafraid to tell a partner when you are dissatisfied with something. Your mutual guarantee actually is "No surprises: if I'm dissatisfied or unhappy, I'll let you know and give us both a chance to correct it. If we can't, then we get help, and if that doesn't fix it, then we renegotiate what we'll do about the relationship."

This is a realistic, sustainable commitment that you can actually expect to meet, and gives you the best possible chance of success. is sustainable and lasting because it contains none of the problems that cause most relationships to break up. Instead of fighting, you work together; instead of feeling deprived, both of you feel fulfilled; instead of frustration, you find solutions; instead of defeat you experience success.

In short, happy partners have a sustainable relationship for the following reason: Why would anyone want to leave a relationship in which can work together to get what they want anytime, even if their wants change as the years go by?

The power of cooperation and negotiation is that it is completely flexible and applicable to almost any possible relationship situation. By learning to use it well, you'll be doing the most you can do to guarantee the success of your relationship, and to maximize your pleasure in sharing your lives together.

Your new skills of communication and negotiation can help you create a partnership that you can sustain over a lifetime together. There are hundreds of books with good and bad ideas about how to make a relationship better. There are trainers, therapists and workshops with methods to use to make your marriage last, from first-aid for little problems to major surgery for the big ones. But the fact is, no matter how good your intentions, it's up to you to make it work. If you keep your relationship easy and rewarding enough, you will do what is necessary to make it work voluntarily and without resentment, even when things change.

Don and Dale found that, as job and financial circumstances changed, their living arrangement had to change, also, and they negotiated to work it out amiably.

Like most couples, John and Rose had tried to adapt to what they thought was a good relationship model: John went to work and earned the money, Rose took care of the house and children, and it suited them until the children grew up. Suddenly, their old relationship focus changed, and Rose felt lost, unneeded and dissatisfied. Using Cooperative Negotiation, Rose and John explored the problem and came up with a new solution and a new focus. When John retired, it also presented many new situations and changes for them to handle.

In this way, negotiation is a basic tool which you and your partner can use to create a relationship at the outset that is sustainable (because it takes into consideration your individual wants and needs) and also to recreate and modify your relationship to suit yourselves as life presents new situations, and as your experience of life changes your attitudes and priorities. By honoring your differences and negotiating each new situation as it arises, you can create a relationship that changes and grows with you, and is as original as you are.

Your Sustainable Relationship

Couples sometimes hesitate to discuss their hopes and dreams because they are afraid that their differences will be insurmountable, and they are basically incompatible. While it's true that two people with widely divergent life goals may have difficulty, and it may even be wiser to seek out more compatible partners, those cases are rare. A couple equipped with the ability to discuss their differences as a team more often discovers that acknowledging and finding ways to accommodate divergent goals adds zest to their partnership.

Expectations and Dreams

Wishing for an unrealistically ideal relationship begins with longing to find someone who will satisfy the unfulfilled cravings for attention, approval, companionship, support and love that may have been left unsatisfied since we were children.

If you or your partner felt your parents were not meeting your needs for nurturing, structure and guidance, you may have yearned for someone to rescue you from disappointment, despair, misery or discomfort. At the same time, you can fear that no one will ever meet your needs, or that you are unworthy. You formulate our hopes and fears about relationships from these unconscious feelings.

New love, in its stew of lust, adrenaline, excitement, exaltation, love, admiration, hope, harmony, laughter, suspense, despair, sensual pleasure, and joy seems automatically and effortlessly to fulfill all your expectations. But soon, the first rush is over, reality sets in and the work begins. If you and your partner begin believing that you'll live happily ever after in an effortless state of bliss, this natural subsiding of infatuation and confrontation with the reality of each other often seems to confirm your fears that love won't work, and lead to disappointment, pain and dissatisfaction.

To give your relationship the solid foundation it needs to last, you must be realistic about what love is, what a partnership is, and what you can reasonably expect of yourself and your partner over an extended period of time. Since most people underestimate what a couple can accomplish together, you may find yourself pleasantly surprised.

A relationship model based on realistic analysis of who you are, what you want and what your circumstances are can be every bit as exciting and satisfying (more so, because you can actually accomplish it) as your wildest fantasy. What is realistic will vary from couple to couple, will change with varying circumstances, and will also depend to some degree on what each of you wants in your relationship. You can have happiness, satisfaction, excitement, and fulfillment, even though life and relationships aren't effortless and perfect.

Expectations are not wrong in themselves. You wouldn't get into a relationship without some expectations or hopes about what will happen. Especially when you are facing your first living together relationship, these expectations can be quite unrealistic. But even people who have been in love before can have expectations that this relationship will be better than the last, or even just like one they had before. Such expectations can be unrealistically positive or unrealistically negative. Either way, when your real-life situation fails to meet your expectations, you can be thrown into confusion and disappointment. A disappointing relationship can be too hard to sustain.

On the other hand, if you have realistic expectations based on reasonable estimates of your own likes, dislikes and abilities, your partner's likes, dislikes and abilities, and the real circumstances life can present; you are prepared to handle most situations in advance. While none of us can predict exactly what life will hold, we can make reasonable estimates that minimize disappointment. This makes your relationship easier to manage, and gives you a much better ability to choose an appropriate partner, and make viable decisions, all of which makes life and relationship more fun.

Exercise: Your Ideal Happy Partnership

This is an opportunity for each of you to explore your dreams and fantasies about love and relationships:

1. Imagine your fantasy relationship:

Imagine living happily ever after, as in a fairy tale or romantic movie. Of all the movies, books, plays and TV shows you've seen, of all the couples you've known, read or heard about, what kinds of relationships are most attractive to you? Allow your fantasy it to be as romantic, sexual, extravagant or simple and quiet as you wish, without criticism. Once you've envisioned your fantasy clearly enough, write it down, and go on to the next step.

2. Set the stage for negotiation:

Set the stage, as in the Negotiation Guide. Make sure you have an uninterrupted time and place, and establish your good feelings for one another to create an atmosphere of cooperation and warmth. Also have an agreement to negotiate.

3. Compare your ideal relationships:

Compare your descriptions of ideal relationships from the previous exercise, either by reading your descriptions out loud, or by exchanging your written descriptions.

4. Look for similarities:

Share first what you like about your partner's ideal relationship, and then ask your partner to do the same. Write on a joint list any characteristics of Happy Partnership that are in both your descriptions.

5. Clarify:

If there are items on your partner's list that you don't agree with or don't understand, ask for more information and paraphrase what your partner tells you (active listening) until you are sure you understand them the way they were intended.

6. List discussion topics:

Make a separate list of items you may disagree or need to negotiate on, and set up a time to do that.

7. Design a model that works for both of you:

Review the mutually agreeable aspects from your ideal relationship lists and discuss what you like about them, and how you can picture your future if they are actualized. Save the lists you've been working with, and use them whenever you feel your relationship needs to be recharged or renegotiated.

Happy Partnership = Sustainable Relationship

Through learning and working together, you will be able to create a sustainable relationship, one that suits both the realities of your life and the real needs and individual differences of you and your partner. It is sustainable because, through negotiation and teamwork, you and your partner create an atmosphere of mutual respect and satisfaction, in which neither of you is prevented from doing what you most want to do.

Although learning a whole new way of relating to each other can be difficult, it is well worth the effort. We urge you to keep using the techniques you have learned here until they become automatic and easy for you, because the rewards are well worth the effort:

- As happy partners, you will feel supported by each other.
- You will always have help and companionship in the hard places.
- You will feel a sense of purpose.
- You will know most of the advantages and reasons you are together.
- You will have goals to work toward, and successes to celebrate.
- When you have failures, you'll also have solace and mutual reassurance.
- You'll feel empowered, because two people, pulling together, have more power than two people pulling separately.
- You'll have the comfort of home with one another.
- You'll know you are allies who will comfort and support one another.
- You'll have a place to feel safe, a place to rest and recuperate.
- You'll have the strength of commitment that comes from knowing that you and your partner are in the best relationship possible for each of you.

And, the beauty of it all is that this partnership can take any form that you and your partner want to give it.

The power of cooperation and negotiation is that it is completely flexible and applicable to almost any possible relationship situation. If you learn to use it well, you'll be doing the most you can do to guarantee the success of your happy partnership, and to maximize your pleasure in your relationship and in your lives together

About the Authors

Tina B. Tessina, Ph.D. www.tinatessina.com is a licensed psychotherapist in S. California since 1978 with over 35 years' experience in counseling individuals and couples and author of 14 books in 17 languages, including *How to Be a Couple and Still Be Free; It Ends With You: Grow Up and Out of Dysfunction; The Ten Smartest Decisions a Woman Can Make After Forty; Love Styles: How to Celebrate Your Differences, The Real 13th Step* and her newest, *Dr. Romance™'s Guide to Finding Love Today.* She writes the "Dr. Romance™" blog, and the "Happiness Tips from Tina" email newsletter. Online, she's known as "Dr. Romance™" Dr. Tessina appears frequently on radio, TV, video and podcasts

Connect with Dr. Tessina online:

Dr. Romance Blog: drromance.typepad.com

Twitter.com/tinatessina

Facebook.com/TinaTessina

Facebook.com/TheReal13thStep

Riley K. Smith, M.A., http://www.rileyksmithmft.com/ is a Licensed Marriage and Family Therapist who has been helping couples and individuals create satisfying relationships since 1974. He supervises and trains therapists in addition to his psychotherapy practice. He is co-author of *How to Be a Couple and Still Be Free, True Partners,* and *Equal Partners*

Other Books by the Authors

By Tina B. Tessina

The Real 13th Step: Discovering Confidence, Self-Reliance and Independence Beyond the Twelve Step Programs Digital Parchment Services 2015 ISBN 13: 978-1615089963

It Ends with You: Grow Up and Out of Dysfunction 2nd edition Muffinhaven Publishing 2014 ISBN-10 149733070X ISBN 13: 978-149733702;

The Ten Smartest Decisions a Woman Can Make After Forty 2nd edition Muffinhaven Publishing 2014 ISBN-10: 1494842033   ISBN-13: 978-1494842031

Love Styles: How to Celebrate Your Differences 2nd edition Muffinhaven Publishing 2011 ISBN-10: 1463783531 ISBN-13: 978-1463783532

Money, Sex and Kids: Stop Fighting about the Three Things That Can Ruin Your Marriage Adams Media 2008 ISBN #1-59869-325-5 256 pages, trade paper, list $12.95

The Commuter Marriage: Keep Your Relationship Close While You're Far Apart Adams Media 2008 ISBN: 1-59869-432-4 220 pages, trade paper, list $14.95

Gay Relationships: How to Find Them, How to Improve Them, How to Make Them Last New Revised edition Tarcher/Putnam 2003. ISBN# 0-87477-566-3. 228 pages trade paper, list $14.95 original edition Tarcher 1988

The Unofficial Guide to Dating Again Wiley, NY 2002 ISBN: 0-02-862454-8, 385 pages trade paper list $16.99 (OOP)

By Riley K. Smith and Tina B. Tessina

How to Be a Couple and Still Be Free 4th Edition ISBN: 1-56414-549-2,

200 pages (co-author Riley K. Smith) Trade paper, list $14.95 Fumbled Book Press, Oakland, CA

True Partners: An Inner Workbook Tarcher 1993 Paperback: 217 ISBN-10: 0874777275 ISBN-13: 978-0874777277 (OOP)

Equal Partners: How to Build a Lasting Relationship Hodder & Stoughton, 1994 ISBN-10: 0340602775 ISBN – 13: 978-0340602775 (OOP)

By Tina B. Tessina, and Elizabeth Friar Williams

The 10 Smartest Decisions A Woman Can Make Before 40 HCI, Deerfield Beach, 1998 ISBN: 1-55-874614-5, 200 pages Trade paper, list $10.95 (12 foreign language editions)

Made in the USA
Middletown, DE
04 April 2022

63596452R00129